Praise for *I, a Squealer*

"Good folks are rarely permitted behind the dark curtain of crime into the inner sanctum of evil where deeply flawed souls lurk. That's what makes Richard Bruns' intimate true-crime memoir so striking and memorable. It is a journey along the razor's edge of morality inside the criminal psyche, where few answers are black-and-white, but all deathly gray. Take a deep breath before you start."

    –Ron Franscell, bestselling author of *The Darkest Night* and Edgar-nominated *Morgue: A Life in Death*

"I have never read a story quite like *I, a Squealer*. This is a true story written in 1967 by Richard Bruns, a young man who became friends with a man in his neighborhood who later committed multiple murders as a serial killer nicknamed 'The Pied Piper of Tucson.' *I, a Squealer* is a first-person look at Bruns' battle with his conscience, his fears and the stigma against ratting on a friend—a powerful and intimate exploration of one man's moral dilemma."

    –Diane Fanning, Edgar Award finalist author of 14 true crime books

"In 1965 the charismatic serial killer Charles Schmid, the 'Pied Piper of Tucson,' gathered around him a group of teens to whom he bragged about his killings and sometimes even showed them the bodies of his victims. One of them was Richard Bruns who eventually went to the police and later testified against Schmid. After the trial and conviction of Schmid, Bruns wrote his inside account of the murders but never published it. Now, fifty years later, Bruns' shocking manuscript has been released to the public giving us for the first time a valuable look into the 'Pied Piper of Tucson' Serial murders in 1964-1965."

    –Peter Vronsky, author of *Serial Killers: the Method and Madness of Monsters* and *Sons of Cain: A History of Serial Killers From the Stone Age to the Present*

"*I, a Squealer* is a gripping and compulsive read that takes you on a twisted ride through the mind of a serial killer and the sinister murders he committed. Hold on tight."

    –RJ Parker, PhD, author of 25 true crime | *The Serial Killers Encyclopedia*

"It is refreshing to find someone who believes that the Schmids of this world, tragic though may be their contributions to life, are potential assets not insects. If people were to carefully study and chronicle these misfits, we might learn something. I beat that drum best I could in the Desalvo (Boston Strangler) case, but no one was listening. Same applies to Schmid."

–F. Lee Bailey, retired defense attorney and author of
The Defense Never Rests

"Nothing I've read about Charles Schmid brings him and his crimes to life in the way this book does. Bruns' account of how he summoned the courage to come forward and confront this charismatic and frightening man is gripping and moving. *I, a Squealer* is a riveting and beautifully written memoir, full of suspense, touches of poetry, and sharp, well-observed details that provide a new and illuminating perspective on a terrible crime. It is both a cautionary tale, told by someone who was dangerously close to a disturbed killer, and a chilling evocation of a dark moment in our history."

–Emily Ross, award-winning author of *Half in Love with Death*

"Bruns chronicles the unraveling of his friend's mental state and documents the outcome in a gripping story that holds you captive until the end. The re-telling of the Schmid murder spree from an insider's view makes this a must-read for not only true crime readers, but all those interested in the inner workings of a ravaged mind and the wide net of horrors it can cast."

–Marla Bernard, retired police sergeant and author of
Through the Rain, A True Crime Memoir of Murder and Survival

"A well-written, interesting, and exciting true crime story!"

–Wayne E. Beyea, author of *Reflections From the Shield*

"An account of the notorious Schmid murders of 1964-65, as told not by a reporter or through hearsay, but by an actual acquaintance of the killer who, after struggling with his conscience, turned Schmid in. Bruns' memoir may be unique in the annals of true crime writing."

–Keven Mcqueen, author of *The Axman Came from Hell,*
Louisville Murder and Mayhem, and *Mayhem in Indiana*

"Charles Schmid is Arizona's most infamous serial killer. Known as the 'Pied Piper of Tucson,' Schmid possessed the uncanny ability to lure teenage girls into the desert and to their deaths. Written by his close companion, Richard Bruns, *I, a Squealer* provides rare insight into the pathology of a psychopath in the midst of his killing spree. Such accounts are rare and of immense value to students of deviant human nature. Though not a professional writer, Bruns presents a compelling account of murder and murderer, and provides at least partial answers to the nagging question of how anyone can commit such terrors. A must read."

–Ronald J. Watkins, author of *Evil Intentions,*
Against Her Will, and many others

"This is Richard Bruns' account of how three girls were murdered. His account of how Charles Howard Schmid Jr. murdered them. And his account of how Schmid forced Bruns to finally come forward to the police, show them two rotting bodies, and tell a story which ultimately sent Schmid to Death Row. Read it and then ask yourself... what you would have done, really now? It's easy to observe and rationalize today, looking back. But put yourself right there with him, and I ask: who would believe you?"

–Michael Gerald Grant, Arizona writer and photographer

"A powerful and chilling first-person true account of the 1964-65 Schmid murders. *I, a Squealer* is an extraordinary and thought-provoking look inside the mind of a serial killer told by Richard Bruns as he struggled through fear, torment, and ultimately turned Charles Schmid into the authorities."

–Kim Cresswell, author of the True Crime Quickie Series

"*I, a Squealer* immerses the reader into the crazy-making world of psychopaths. In his firsthand account, Richard Bruns shares his involvement with Charles H. Schmid, Jr., the convicted murderer from 1960's Tucson. Mr. Bruns brilliantly details how easy it is to get tangled in a psychopath's web and how hard it is to escape."

–Barbara Bentley, author of *A Dance with the Devil: A True*
Story of Marriage to a Psychopath

"A gripping eye-witness, behind-the-scenes account of a notorious murder spree from the mid-'60s, an event that marked Tucson's passage from a small innocent town to a large, violent city."

    –Dave Devine, author of *Tucson: A History of the Old Pueblo From the 1854 Gadsden Purchase*

"This book is a rare opportunity to understand from a first-person perspective what happens when a serial killer entangles an innocent person in his madness and crimes. Well-written and powerful, it's a tale of good and bad I'm not likely to forget."

    –Trudy J. Smith, author of *The Meaning of Our Tears*

"*I, a Squealer* is a riveting true story of one man's struggle to do the right thing. Richard Bruns takes the reader on an emotional journey as he faces his darkest fears to help police catch a killer—a killer he personally knows and knows well. This book is well worth the read, and I highly recommend it to anyone who loves true crime books."

    –Deb, TrueCrimeDiva.com

"I read *I, a Squealer* with a great interest as it provided me with a view of a serial killer's behavior and interactions with others that, as a forensic scientist, I do not glean from a crime scene. The personal account given by Richard Bruns of his companionship with serial killer, Charles Schmid, offers a powerful insight into the complexities and uncertainties he endured with this evil person. This book is well-written and Bruns shares many fascinating details of his interactions with the 'Pied Piper of Tucson.'"

    –Stuart H. James, forensic consultant

"Most people who get this first-hand peek into a serial killer's mind wind up as victims; Richard Bruns has done a fantastic job of bringing us right into the insanity of his circumstances. I just wish he knew more killers so we could get some other books from him… but with his lively writing style, I'd settle for fiction too."

    –Jeff Klima, author of *The Dead Janitors Club*

"I, a Squealer is a truly chilling story!"

    –David Hanna, author of *Rendezvous with Death*

I, a Squealer

THE Insider's Account of the "Pied Piper of Tucson" Murders

Richard Bruns

ISBN: 978-0-9831665-5-9

Library of Congress Control Number
LCCN: 2017908999

cover photo: gettyimages.com / The LIFE Picture Collection / Bill Ray
cover and interior design: the RBDI group, LLC / Aimée Carbone

Published by
Twin Feather Publishing
PO Box 18910
Tucson, AZ 85731

Dedication

To my daughter Lisa for her
passion and commitment to this book.

About This Book

The manuscript for this book was written in 1967 by Richard Bruns, the man who blew the whistle on Charles Schmid, resulting in Schmid's arrest and conviction for multiple murders in Tucson, Arizona. This is Richard's account of what happened.

At the time of the writing, Richard was married and had a brand new baby girl, and he was ready to close this chapter of his life. The manuscript was packed away, like a time capsule, not to be seen again until forty years later when his three daughters were looking through old photos and came across it. After reading it, his daughter Lisa urged Richard to put it out into the world so that his side of the story could finally be shared. He was reluctant. The manuscript was returned to him, and more time passed. Years later, when his daughters asked him about it again, he explained that it was misplaced and he might have accidentally thrown it out. His daughters were devastated that this piece of their father's history might be lost forever.

Then, in 2015, when his daughters were helping him to move, they searched in hopes of finding the lost manuscript. When it was once again discovered, they were thrilled and quickly took it for safekeeping.

When word got out that yet another book on the subject was due to be published, they urged their father to share his side of the story. This time, tired of always being portrayed in books and articles as someone he wasn't, Richard agreed.

This isn't a book of memories distorted after years of passing. Rather, this was written over fifty years ago when Richard was twenty years old and the events were fresh and vivid in his mind. Many books and articles have shared the Charles Schmid murder cases, but none have been from an insider. Here, Richard takes you into the scenes and events from a view never seen or heard before, shedding new light on the murders that shocked the nation and changed the city of Tucson forever.

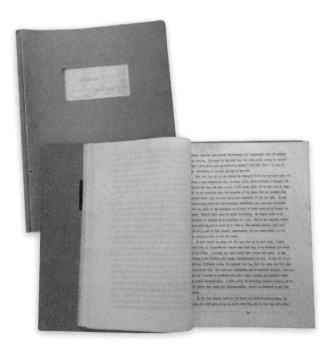

Original manuscript, written in 1967

Contents

Introduction

Two pair of hands, then three. The crowd—adults, teenagers, little kids seven and eight years old—looked on anxiously as the officers went about their gruesome task.

Each was giving the other instructions:

"Careful."

"Carefully."

Another man knelt close by with a microphone to record the dialogue. Half a dozen cameras clicked, and there was a steady buzz from a movie camera.

"Where's the refreshments?" one man asked loudly, laughing.

A few people turned to look his way, but only a few, and only for a quick moment. Then they turned back, enveloped deeply in the "show" taking place.

"Be careful with the cranium," Schmid was recorded as saying. "It's delicate. It can prove my innocence."

The men worked cautiously, digging and brushing the dirt away from the now-distinguishable object.

A little girl tugged at her fathers coat. "Daddy, where's her leg?" she asked.

I

I, a Squealer

Charles Schmid's manacled hands unearthing the skull of Alleen Rowe
Grasberger / Tucson Daily Citizen

Introduction

He knelt down to her line of sight and pointed.

Then a single camera clicked, and the result was a story of a million words. In its center—a human skull. Around it, clutching it, was a pair of manacled hands.

"Be careful with the cranium," he emphasized again, "Its delicate."

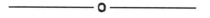

Silently, the jury re-entered the courtroom and took their places at the jury box.

"We find the defendant, Charles Howard Schmid Jr.—"

Please, please.

"Guilty…."

Oh, no, Smitty! No, no!

"….of murder in the first degree."

Schmid sat expressionless as the verdict was read, while his wife Diane cried uncontrollably.

It's not right, I thought when I heard the guilty verdict announced on the radio. Why didn't his lawyer plead him insane? He doesn't belong there. He's sick.

As famed defense attorney Percy Foreman would later say of the verdict, "The lawyer should accept at least part of the blame." He was probably wondering himself why William Tinney hadn't pleaded Schmid insane. "It would have made a great case for an insanity defense."

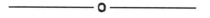

I, a Squealer

"I just sit here in my cell, and I look out the window at the little building over there—the gas chamber—and I wonder if I'm going to die. Someday, after I'm dead, there'll be another murder, and then everyone will say, 'Gee, we're awfully sorry Smitty. We made a mistake. But you're already dead, so there isn't anything we can do about it.' It is my belief and contention that Richard Bruns is the murderer...

Richard Bruns is the murderer."

1

Smitty

I am Richard Bruns, the person that turned Smitty—Charles Howard Schmid Jr.—into the police, and in his mind, to the gas chamber of the Arizona State Prison. I would have never believed it would end that way. I felt then, and still do feel, that he was without control of his actions—because he was sick.

I was a witness to him losing his mind. Like the time he grabbed his cat, tied a heavy cord to its tail, and began to bash it bloody against the wall. It howled such high-pitched, penetrating screams that I thought my eardrums would burst, as over and over again he bashed it into the wall, until finally the contents of its bowels began to seep out. Then he turned to me, his eyes searching deep behind my own, as though by straining he could see right through me, and said, almost in a whisper, "You feel compassion. Why?"

I was afraid to stay there alone with him. I knew what he was capable of doing. I just got the hell out of there.

It was six months earlier when he told me of how he killed a teenage schoolgirl just to see what it felt like. We were hanging out at a city park, just shooting the bull and passing time, when he described to me the uncontrollable urge he had to kill someone, anyone, and how he and another friend, John Saunders, had walked the streets together searching for a possible victim and the right opportunity.

When the opportunity didn't present itself after a week or so of prowling, he called up Mary French, his steady at the time, and gave her a list containing the names of three girls. She was supposed to persuade one to sneak away from home with them, supposedly go out into the desert to drink beer.

The list was a death list. A pretty young girl named Alleen Rowe, the third name on the list, became the victim. In every minute detail I remembered his account of the murder, and I doubted I would ever forget it. It had become the basis for my recurring nightmare—the damned, horrifying thing that haunted me every time I closed my eyes.

Even Paul G. had grown afraid of him. Paul was a childhood friend of Smitty's who himself had murdered at the age of fifteen. The victim, an Air force colonel, was shot through the head during a bungled robbery attempt. Paul spent five years in a reformatory for the killing.

"What happened?" I asked Paul after he shared his fear of Smitty.

"I just asked him what in the hell he was doing messing around with a fourteen year old girl, that Diane, and he told me it wasn't none of my damned business and blew up. He slammed his goddamned fist through the wall, and then went running around outside in his underwear, jumping back and forth over the fence screaming, 'God is going to punish me.

God is going to punish me.' He's really cracked up. I know he killed Gretchen and Wendy. Are you sure he didn't tell you anything about it?"

"No, he didn't tell me anything," I lied. "He didn't say anything at all about it." But the truth was he had told me everything.

I was sitting with Smitty in his small cottage home when he shared the details of the murders. He calmly turned to me and said, "I've killed four times, not three. Now it's your turn to kill someone, Richie." He said it so threateningly. "Now it's your turn to kill someone, Richie." It echoes through my mind even now.

I lit a cigarette and our eyes met.

He's flipped. He was not the same Smitty I grew up with.

He got up and put an Elvis Presley record on his old phonograph then walked to the refrigerator.

"You want a beer?" he asked.

"No thanks," I responded.

He pulled out a gallon jug of home-brewed beer, poured himself a glass of it, and then returned to the living room, where he sat down across from me on the couch.

The phone rang. A few weeks earlier, if the phone had rung, it would have been a cause for alarm, but now, whenever it rang, there was no panic because he knew she wasn't at the other end of the line. She was dead.

I lit another cigarette, took a long drag, and began to look around the room as he talked into the phone. For the first time since I had seen his place the drapes and the door were open, letting some daylight in, and for the first time I wasn't overcome

Schmid's Cottage Home / Getty Images

with that depressing feeling of being locked away in some dark hole of a cave. Nothing inside had changed, but at least it seemed alive now.

There were magazines strewn about on the floor, along with records, clothes, pillows, dirty bed sheets, and dirtied glasses and plates with bits of uneaten food still on them. Some of them had been sitting there for as long as a week. They were scattered wherever they could be piled. The rest of the dishes were in the kitchen. The odor in there was overwhelming, like a sewer.

Next to me was the dining room table. It was covered with blotches of dripped wax from when Smitty had sat there and painstakingly made candleholders from wine bottles. The table itself was in shreds from his continued hacking on it with a machete, as was the arm of the chair in which I was sitting. The tree out in the front yard had also received the same treatment.

On the opposite wall, straight across from me, was a hole he had made with his fist in a fit of rage. It gave mute but frightening testimony to the power chained inside his small, compact body, and of the damage he was capable of inflicting when he unleashed that power in just one unmerciful blow. It caused me to recall what he had done to his cat, the lack of mercy he had shown it, and I shuddered. I knew that he was totally without mercy.

He hung up the phone and there was a long silence. Smitty was the first one to speak, but he spoke as though he were talking only to himself.

"If I'm ever caught," he began, "I'll never confess. That way they'd never know, and the not knowing would torture them."

I, a Squealer

He sat back into the couch and pondered what he had just said, and smiled. *It would torture them.* That was clearly important to him.

He fixed his eyes squarely on the floor and sank into deep thought. I immediately seized the opportunity to study him for a moment, this person I feared so much but to whom I was bound so closely by circumstance. I was three years younger than Smitty. We had met through Paul G. nearly five years earlier. In a brief flashback I recalled the Smitty I used to know, the Smitty who used to be my friend a long time ago. That Smitty had been completely different from the guy sitting across from me now. As I compared the two, I wondered how it was possible he could have degenerated so much.

Once he had been the cool leader of the Tucson's teenage set —the teenager's champion, their idol, their hero. I was younger then, and I myself had idolized him. Now, although he was still their king, he was becoming incapable of leading anyone. No more, as it had been in 1960 when I'd first met him, did the teenage throngs mull and crowd about him in public just to be near him, to be a part of him, to drink in the mysterious strength he generated to them, and to revel in that strength of rebellion.

By the hundreds they had once flocked to him. He never had to utter the least little word or command. The communication between them had been almost telepathic. At the same time it was dangerously real and undeniably strong. The power he held over Tucson's youth could hardly be exaggerated—he had since been appropriately labeled "The Pied Piper of Tucson."

Once he had all the things the typical teenager lived for and held dear—money, a new convertible car, clothes, looks, dates at the snap of his fingers, and even a rock and roll band. Now he had none of that. All that remained were fragments of the myth that had been created about him, and even those were dying out fast.

At twenty-three years old, he was becoming more and more alienated from the world of the teenager, a world he could never allow himself to leave. Without that world he would be nothing. No longer would he be glorified or thought of as something of a god. He was steadily losing touch with it, and he knew it. "I'm on the outside looking in," he once told me, and he felt himself experiencing his own destruction. He was falling victim to his own image.

While we sat, he sensed my gaze, and his eyes rose up to meet mine. I blew smoke from my cigarette and turned away from him. He returned his stare to the floor. I paused and then looked back toward him again. He was sitting there fondling his glass, thumb-tapping its rim. He was off in an entirely different world, far removed from me, from the room, and from anything around him. His eyes were bloodshot, and he appeared drugged. How and why had I become so involved with him? I asked myself. I felt guilty of something terrible because of it.

He was an aberrant man, to say the least. In his high topped boots stuffed with as many rags, tin cans, and whatever he could make fit, he put an additional three inches of height on his stubby five-foot, three-inch frame. He clomped around in those boots as though he were going to topple at every step. Whenever he was asked about it, he explained that he had swollen ankles, and that was why his boots were so fat and clunky. I thought he looked like he was wearing Santa Claus boots. Some people actually thought he had wooden feet. It no longer mattered to him that he looked like a clown, just as long as he didn't look small.

He worked so hard to create an exaggerated persona that he went a bit overboard. On his left cheek he had painted a beauty mark. What had started out the size of a pinhole was now the size of a quarter. On his nose he wore a bandage caked with grit. Two months earlier he claimed he had gotten into a fight and broke his nose and the bandage was what remained of the episode. He wore white lipstick to accent the dark complexion he had acquired by gulping suntan pills, sitting for hours under a sun lamp, and applying liquid makeup to his skin. His light brown hair was dyed jet black and then combed into a pompadour. Even the hairs on his arms and chest had been dyed, and daily he did touch-up work on his eyelashes and eyebrows.

Everything about him was imitation, and all of it his own creation—even his mannerisms. These he carefully practiced to perfection by standing in front of a mirror for hours at a time, pursing his lips and emulating whoever he'd have himself be. Yet, ironically, he'd become quite good at winning over other people's confidence, and people trusted him fully.

On many occasions I listened to him as he laughed and told me story after story on the gullibility of people, and time and again I'd seen him prove that gullibility. Most everyone he ever came into contact with fell head over heals for his crazy, unbelievable lines.

There was the one where he had leukemia and didn't have long to live. He told others that he had a bad heart that was expected to give out at any second. And then there was the ultimate in stories in which he described how, when he was a baby, he had to be put into a stretching machine because he had been stunted at birth.

He bragged to me that he had learned every con there was from an old acquaintance of his, and he had used those tricks with a considerable amount of success to get money and whatever else he wanted. For a time he had also received a three-hundred-dollar-a-month allowance and credit card access from his parents, who were proprietors of a million-dollar nursing home. Of course, that was before. Now the nursing home was in receivership. When it went away, so did the allowance and credit cards. Now, Smitty was left with just the little home in which we were sitting.

He still attempted to use his conning techniques on his mother. When he wanted money to go to California to cut a record and lay his claim to fame, he sent Mary French to her with a story about being pregnant by Smitty and needing twenty-five dollars. His mother refused to give it to her. Undoubtedly she recalled the other story Smitty and Mary had told her about getting secretly married in Texas—a ploy Smitty had used so that he and Mary could sleep together in her home—and the various other times she had let Smitty con her out of something with his swift talk. He even had her believing once that he was attending classes at the university, when all of the time he was really at a restaurant eating pancakes with me and wasn't even enrolled in the university. But that time, naturally, his mom had paid him extra money for going to school.

His biggest mistake, and his biggest let down later, was that he believed he could go on conning the same people indefinitely without anyone ever catching on. But even his mother had reached a point with him. It proved him to be the biggest fool of all.

He was completely incapable of telling the truth, I concluded, or of projecting his true emotions and feelings. He insisted that the world was phony and deceitful, and so in order to beat the world at its own game he had decided to become more phony than the whole lot. Over time he did just that. In fact, he had played the part so well for so long that now he seemed to be hovering somewhere on the brink of schizophrenia—unaware, and more unsure than ever, as to just exactly who he really was and what he stood for. He only knew what he didn't stand for: Conformity, society, God, and everything else that attempted to dictate his actions. He once even tore up a Bible, page by page, and burned it in the street in front of my house. With nothing to do now but roam in search of pleasure in any form he could find it, time had won out in the end. What was sitting across from me now was the product of non-purposefulness.

The one factor that made him more dangerous than ever was his ability to convey a feeling of trust between himself and others. He had impeccable manners, and he could, if he wanted, move in even the best of circles. While some parents refused to let their children associate with many nice and harmless boys, turning them away at their doors, Smitty himself was seldom turned away. Whenever he was in the presence of parents he projected an image of the All-American boy, and with his witty humor and kind gestures he could be quite irresistible. Some adults thought of him as a big brother to their children, mostly

Smitty

because their children appeared to respect him. These same adults felt they could use Smitty and his influence to reach their offspring. Some, in fact, turned to Smitty for advice and direction. It was ironic.

"Do you have a cigarette, Richie?" Smitty asked.

"Yeah," I replied and reached inside my shirt pocket for one.

He got up and came over to me for the cigarette, lit it, handed me back my book of matches, and then turned to the phonograph again to put on his favorite Elvis record, "They Remind me Too much of You." It was his song to her. A song with a past, and with a memory fiery and tender. At one time he had loved her, but now she was dead and he was glad. He was relieved and finally at ease. He just didn't care anymore. He was past caring.

"I guess you know what happened to Gretchen," he said to me.

I said "yes" because by then there was so little doubt in my mind. He had told me of Alleen Rowe who he had killed with the help of John Saunders. He had even tried to coax me to rape and murder with him to help him wipe out an entire family. He was to have "taken care of" the mother and father, and I was to have "taken care of" the brother and sister, and then he'd planned to rape and kill a couple of girls in California. He was serious; I knew that, just as I knew he had been serious when he repeatedly told me he would someday kill Gretchen. When she turned up missing with her younger sister, Wendy, I surmised what had happened.

Now he was confirming my suspicions—confessing it all. "First I killed Gretchen, and Wendy was still going 'huh-huh-

11

I, a Squealer

SPECIAL

Police *Tucson* Bulletin

P. O. BOX 1071
TUCSON POLICE DEPARTMENT
TUCSON, ARIZONA

Bernard L. Garmire
CHIEF OF POLICE

NORMA ALLEEN ROWE, WAF, DOB 27 October 1948, Dallas, Texas, 120#
blonde hair, brown eyes, fair tanned complexion, white blemish
center of back, small scar right eyebrow, very faint. Missing
since 31 May 1964 at 2230 hours from 7342 Calle Cuernavaca, Tucson,
Arizona. The only clothes at time she left home is a one piece
black bathing suit, blouse with yellow flowers and orange rubber
thongs. Destination unknown.

Any information - Tucson Police Department, Tucson, Arizona,
phone 791-4404 or 791-4411.

Juvenile Detail, Case #276330.

12

huh,' and then I just….

As he revealed the details I wondered if there was something I could have done to prevent it.

"Then I put the bodies into the trunk of her car and drove out and dumped them. I put them in the most obvious place I could get caught—because I just didn't care anymore."

But, tragically, there had been nothing I could do. I couldn't have turned him into the police for murdering Alleen because I didn't know where her body was, and I had no proof. The police had already questioned him regarding her disappearance anyway, and they had no proof either.

If I had told the police about his plans to kill other people and of his threats to kill Gretchen, it would have been my word against his. Then it might have been me ending up dead somewhere out in the desert. Now Gretchen and Wendy were gone and he was claiming that there was yet a fourth victim, but I still had no proof. There was nothing I could do. But I would try. Soon I would be running the streets like a madman, overwrought with terror and compelled by suspicion, trying to keep him from killing again.

"How are you and Kathy getting along?" Smitty asked.

"The same," I answered. I did not elaborate.

He started to talk, paused for a moment, and then said, "Maybe we ought to go get Gretchen and hang her by a noose on Kathy's porch. That ought to bring her around."

Soon after that I departed.

2

Guarding Kathy

Day turned into night, and with the night came restless, tormented sleep. It was always the same nightmare, and by now I felt like I was losing my mind from it. It had driven me to the verge of a breaking point, and it was obvious I couldn't go on for much longer.

On this night, as on so many other nights before it, I found myself abruptly sitting up in bed, staring off into the darkness. I was breathing hard, and my heart was throbbing. Perspiration drenched my forehead, and scenes of horror filled my eyes. Just seconds before I had been engulfed in a race against death to save another's life, and now, suddenly, and with a loud cry of anguish, there was only pitch black everywhere.

At my first conscious moment, it seemed to me that this was death, and there was an icy coldness about it. My body trembled and my mind whirled in circles trying to catch up with all that was happening. After a few long moments I managed to return to reality. It was only that bad dream, I thought. I exhaled deeply and sank back down onto the pillow. I lay there thinking, What is this insane madness?

I, a Squealer

It had begun two months earlier while I was still dating a girl named Kathy. A prowler had been coming by her bedroom window at night, making whispering sounds and messing with her screen. Kathy was terrified. She told me what was happening, and, enraged, I set out to catch the person in the act.

One night I parked my car down the street from her house and waited for him to show. Hours passed by without so much as a glimpse of anyone. Finally, just as I was preparing to give up, Smitty appeared on the scene. His gold Ford Falcon Sprint turned the corner onto the block from the opposite end of where I was and slowly cruised past Kathy's house with its lights out. It appeared as though he was going to stop, but then he saw me and nonchalantly drove up to start a conversation. He said he was out there at two-thirty in the morning just to look for me.

Smitty had gone with Kathy some time before I had, and it was through him that I'd first met her. They had even been engaged once, theoretically, after he gave her a cheap cut glass ring to bind the engagement. But when he found she was useless to him because she wouldn't go to work as Mary French had done and deposit her earnings into a joint bank account with him, he dropped her. That was when I started dating her.

After encountering him on her street that night, my horrid nightmare began—not so bad at first, but growing in impact and urgency through seemingly endless repetition until, before it was over, it would become much too harsh and painful.

Details of my dream were just like the murder of Alleen Rowe, as Smitty had told it to me, only with Kathy as the victim. And instead of being bludgeoned to death she was slowly being strangled. But the great similarity, most importantly, was the

16

Guarding Kathy

fact that it was Smitty doing the killing.

As for me, I played a role of absolute helplessness. I would be running across an infinite span of desert, gun in hand, to save Kathy but could never get there in time. The harder I ran the more distant they became. It was her face that lingered on and haunted me more than anything. She always looked so helpless, with tears streaming down the sides of her cheeks as he tightened his grip around her throat, and it was that sight that was eating me away from the inside and overpowering my will and senses.

I had become convinced, through torment or reason, that Smitty intended to kill Kathy, and I was obsessed with it. In desperation I took upon myself the task of standing guard over her. I literally made her a prisoner in her own home, and I defied a whole city block in order to do it.

I used fear as my weapon. I stood on corners, and I paraded up and down in front of her house from early in the morning until late at night, day after day. Whenever she left to go somewhere, on her own or with her parents, I followed. I made it clear to her that she was not to go out on any dates or to see any friends away from home—I was a lover scorned, she believed —and my continued presence there enforced my demands on her, not to mention spooking the rest of the neighborhood in the process.

People watched from behind closed doors. Mothers pulled their kids off of the street and forbade them to play. Husbands formed vigilante committees and laid traps for me. They ordered me off of the block and then saw me to its borders, only to find me returning five minutes later, walking a death march down the

17

sidewalk and pounding a baseball bat onto the concrete at every other step. They called the police, and the police threatened to arrest me for loitering. To compromise, I fetched my dog from home and walked it up and down the street, hour after hour. Whenever I was watching her it would become, in a way, a kind of challenge to withstand all of the resistance I was receiving.

With the advent of nightfall everyone's porch light was turned on, and the street was deserted except for when I would occasionally show myself. I imagined that inside every home there was the same conversation: "What's he up to? I wonder where he is. I know he's lurking out there somewhere. All day and all night, whenever I look outside I see him, just standing and watching. For what?"

When school began I took my vigil to Kathy's locker and to her classes. I recruited my friends from around the school to help me, and so her every move was watched, even though the dean of the school had gotten onto my case and had me evicted from the premises. Regularly my spies made reports back to me on her movements; it was like a game to them. I wished to God it could have been a game to me, too.

Whenever I was away from the block, and away from her, my anxiety grew until it became so painful that I had to return. I was compelled to return. I had gotten so distressed that I lost all control over my actions. I had to know where she was every second—to know she was safe—and the only way I could accomplish that was to keep her at home. And I had to apply fear to do it.

Kathy ended up dropping out of school after a short period of time and went into such great seclusion inside her home that

Guarding Kathy

I thought for a while she moved away. It was criminal what I was doing to her, but to this day I believe it saved her life. Smitty went down her street many nights after I started to guard her, always just to "look for" me, and every time he ventured anywhere close to her I had stopped him.

He even thought I was sleeping most nights in the alley across the street, although he wasn't sure why. He wasn't too far wrong. I was the only person in the world that could have crept through that alley and caused the dogs to wag their tails instead of bark; they knew me well enough. Before it was over, I would have remained the area's elusive phantom for well over three-and-a-half long and tortured months.

It was just before I left my house one morning that the phone rang. It was Smitty.

"I'm having a party over at my house tonight. There'll be booze and there should be a lot of girls. You want to come?"

"A party," I repeated.

"Yeah. You want to come?"

"I don't know," I said.

"You haven't got anything better to do," he reminded me.

"Well, yeah. What time is it for?"

"Around seven-thirty."

"Ah, I don't know man," I said.

"Well, why not?"

"I just…."

"Ah, come on. It'll be something for you to do."

"Well….okay, I guess so. Yeah, why not?"

"You'll come then?"

"Yeah, I'll come."

I, a Squealer

"Great. Around seven-thirty?"

"Yeah, I'll be there."

"Okay, we'll see ya tonight then," he said and hung up.

Actually, I was more than willing to go. My only moments of relief came when I was with him because it was then that I didn't have to worry over Kathy. As long as I was with one of the two of them, nothing could happen. But it was seldom I ever saw him anymore.

Since the nursing home had gone into receivership and he had moved to the other side of town, he had made new friends —people I didn't know—and it was almost impossible for me to find him. He was never at home. And so whenever he called to make an appointment, as he had on this day, I considered it a blessing.

Soon after talking to him, I left for Kathy's street, thermos jug and lunch in hand, to take up my sentry duty. First, I stopped the milkman, who assured me he had seen Kathy when he had delivered milk to her house, and then I settled back for my long stay. It was nice to know I'd be leaving early for a change. It was always harder to watch her at night.

At six-thirty I left there, after having convinced myself that everything would be all right. I went home and had some supper, and then had my parents drive me over to Smitty's. I no longer had my own car. I had smashed it into an ice cream truck as I was chasing another car I'd suspected Kathy of being in, trying to give me the slip, and that was the last I'd seen of it, or what was left of it. It was the last I'd see of my driver's license for many years, too.

They dropped me off in front of Smitty's house and left. It

was just before seven-thirty, but it was already dark. There were no cars in front, and as I looked the scene over I became filled with apprehension. It certainly didn't look like there was a party going on. There was an inexplicable quiet all about me. I turned and saw the tail lights of my parents' car disappear as it rounded a corner a block up, and then I turned back to face the house again.

There was one dim light on in the front room, but there were no signs of anyone being present. I began to move slowly up the walkway toward the door. I opened it, looked around inside, and saw that the room was empty. I called out "Smitty," and waited for an answer; there was none. My stomach started to churn; my knees weakened in growing alarm. I walked back out to the road, where I slumped down helplessly onto the curb. A thousand and one thoughts raced through my head.

I was there probably only a short time, but it seemed like an eternity before a car approached. As it got closer, the driver put his bright lights on. The car slowed, pulled over, and then stopped a few feet away. The engine shut off, and the lights died out. The door on the driver's side opened and someone emerged from the car. My eyes were still blinded from the headlights, and so I was unable to make out who it was at first.

"What are you doing out here? Where is everybody? I thought there was supposed to be a party here tonight."

I recognized the voice as that of one of Smitty's newfound friends, a guy I had met briefly and had seen around a couple of times.

"I don't know," I answered. "I was told the same thing."

"How long have you been sitting here?" he asked.

I, a Squealer

"A few minutes, I guess."

He looked toward the house. "Is the door open?"

"Yeah."

"Well, no sense in just standing around," he said and started for the door.

I've been tricked! Oh my God, I know it! He's with Kathy already, luring her off somewhere to kill her!

It was seven miles from there to Kathy's, and my first instinct was to try to run it. But, I reasoned, Smitty might return any second. I might be wrong. I had to stay; I couldn't afford not to know. Although I had to force myself to, I followed him inside.

I sat down while he put a record on the phonograph and checked to see if there was any beer. There wasn't any. After a while, he came over and sat down next to me.

"I wonder where Smitty is."

The door opened and four more people entered, only two of whom I had seen before.

"Where's Smitty?" somebody asked.

"I don't know," I answered.

Everyone sat and gawked at each other. The needle on the phonograph reached the end of a record, but failed to trip. Bla-bloop. Bla-bloop. Someone got up to change it. Sweat poured from my face. I wanted to move, to do something. I couldn't just sit there doing nothing at all, but what could I do? It was such a perfect set up.

The door opened again. I turned to see who it was—two more strangers. They came in and sat down. More time passed. It was getting late.

Again, the door opened. I turned. I waited. *Please.* I clenched

22

my fists as hard as I could. Someone entered and a face came into view. I could hardly believe my eyes at first. The blood rushed back to my head as he walked in. I sighed, and my body grew limp. I collapsed back into the chair. *Thank God. How much of this....just how much more could I take?*

"I'm sorry," Smitty began, "but I had to go away." He started to make the rounds to say hello to everyone.

Two other men, strangers to me, entered directly behind him. They were different—older than anyone else in the room, about Smitty's age. They were dressed in flashy suits, and they were both puffing on long stogies. There was something mysterious about them. They didn't fit there somehow.

They looked around the room and then at me. They eyed each other, and then nodded. One of them blew a smoke ring.

"Richie," someone said. "Richie."

I jumped. "Huh?" I looked up and saw Smitty standing over me.

"Do you want to come out front with me for a minute?"

"Out front?" I repeated, not understanding.

"Yeah." He moved in the direction of the door and motioned for me to follow.

I couldn't think. I was in a stupor. I just looked at him quizzically, got up, and did as I was told. The two men in suits preceded us and walked to a late-model car with New Jersey license plates that was parked in the street.

Smitty stopped me midway on the lawn and told me, "These men are from the Mafia. They want to take us to see some other men. I've already been there. They want to talk to you about Gretchen."

"Mafia!" I exclaimed. "About Gretchen?"

I, a Squealer

"Don't worry," he said. "They won't hurt you."

He led me to the car and herded me into the back seat. It all happened so fast. He climbed in after me, and then the two men got in, and we drove off.

3

The Mafia

We were driven down Speedway Boulevard, Tucson's "action strip," past the drive-ins, night clubs, supermarkets, and gas stations. No one spoke the whole way. I watched the scenery go by and made nervous jokes to myself. I had finally flipped my lid; tonight was the final straw.

We eventually stopped at an apartment building a few blocks off of Speedway, where we were taken out and escorted through an open patio to a small apartment on the ground floor, close to the apartment's swimming pool. We hadn't even been blindfolded, an image I recalled from the gangster movies I'd seen on TV.

Inside the apartment three men were waiting. One of them, a much older man, was sitting on a mattress that pulled out from beneath an oversized corner table, and the other two were sitting in chairs—one facing the older man, and the other facing the bar. I immediately recognized the two in the chairs from the newspapers.

The one facing the bar was Charles "Batts" Battaglia, an

Speedway Boulevard in 1966 / Getty Images

I, a Squealer

alleged underworld figure, and the other was Salvatore Bonanno, oldest son of kingpin Mafia leader Joseph "Joe Bananas" Bonanno of New York. They appeared real enough, but what was I doing there? What did they want with me? I learned later that one of the two men who had driven us there from the party was Joe Bonanno Jr., youngest son of Bonanno.

Smitty sat down on a chair by the door next to Battaglia, and I sat on a stool at the bar as I was directed, putting myself in the limelight. Joe Jr. and the other man with him had left and were out by the swimming pool talking with some women. I relaxed. I figured they wouldn't machine-gun us down there at any rate.

I looked over at the old man. He was massaging his fist, and then he switched over and massaged the other. He pounded it into his palm, caressed his knuckles with his fingers, squeezed in and snapped the bones, and then massaged it some more. He was looking at the leg of the chair Bonanno was sitting in, and he never moved his eyes. He was dressed in flimsy baggy pants, and his shoes resembled something he had removed from a passed-out wino on the street. His shirt looked second-hand, and his grey hair was a mess.

Battaglia had silver-grey hair and fit the perfect gangster stereotype. He was heavyset with a beer gut, and he was cleanly and casually dressed. He had a loud, gruff voice that almost totally concealed his underlying accent, which was more eastern than foreign, and with every word he spoke he gave the impression of being not too bright. He reminded me of a punch-drunk ex-prizefighter, minus all the scar tissue.

Bonanno was the cleanest. He was dressed in tight-fitting

tapered pants with a white form-fitting shirt, and his black hair was neatly combed. He seemed more like a small-time hoodlum than he did a big syndicate gangster, but he did appear threatening. He had his legs crossed and he was smacking his lips, savoring the taste of his beer.

"You're Richard Bruns, huh?" Battaglia popped up.

"Yeah," I answered.

"We brought you here because we wanted to talk to you."

I'd managed to figure that out already. "Yeah," I said.

"You know Gretchen Fritz?"

"Yeah."

"And you know she's missing?"

"Yeah."

"And her sister. What's her name?"

"Wendy," Bonanno said.

"Yeah, Wendy is missing with her," Battaglia said.

"Yes."

"Well, we've been asked by a friend to help find them, and that's why we want to talk to you. We've already talked to Smitty here for a bit, but we wanted to get the two of you together. It seems of all the names that have popped up in the thing that your's and Smitty's are the ones that come out on top of people who should know where they are, and so naturally we wanted to talk to you two first."

"Yeah," I said.

"Now," he began, "I want you to understand that we're not like the cops. We're on opposite ends with them bastards. You want to know what I'm like, you just go ask Garmire, the chief of police, what kind of a son of a bitch I am. He'll tell you. In fact, I've got to go to court here in about three weeks, and I'm facing maybe fifteen years. So anything you tell us won't go past this room. We don't tell the cops nothing, you know. So feel free to tell us anything. If you know something, tell us. You do us a favor, maybe someday we can help you and do you a favor in return.

"Human lives are at stake here," Battaglia continued, "and so we intend to find these girls one way or the other. If we find them dead, or something like that, we just pull out of the thing. Like I said, we don't tell the cops nothing. But if the girls are being held by somebody or they're in some kind of trouble, we want to find them and help them. We don't want to put you on the spot, but if you know something, come clean, that's all."

"I don't know where they are. I don't know where they went," I said. Smitty and I exchanged glances.

"You don't have any idea, not even a hint as to where they are?" Battaglia asked.

"No."

"You're sure?"

"Yes."

"I just don't want you to tell us one thing tonight," he said, "and then later on we find out that you were lying to us. Tell us what you know and you don't have anything to be afraid of."

"I don't know anything," I said emphatically. "I haven't seen Gretchen for ages." And I hadn't. "Maybe they're in California. Smitty thinks they might be."

"I'm sure they are," Smitty interrupted, seeing me getting into trouble. "I just wish I had a way of getting there. I know I could find them."

The Mafia

"You're that sure they're over there?" Battaglia asked him.

"I'm pretty sure they are. Like I told you, Gretchen was there on vacation just a week before she disappeared, and she admitted to finding a boyfriend in San Diego and going out on me. I think she went back over to see him. I've even got the boyfriend's name."

I had been at Smitty's house on the night Gretchen returned to Tucson and called to tell him that she went out on him. He'd stormed from the house, slamming the door. I had gone outside after him and found him pacing the driveway. He knelt beside his car, and burst into tears and cried, "I really loved that girl." I knew then the end was nearing. It was surprising to me it hadn't come much sooner. It had always been a matter of time, but the question had been just how much time.

Battaglia continued his probing. "They were reported to have been seen in Mexico. What about that?"

"Man, you could take their pictures around to any place in the world," Smitty countered, "and find someone to swear they'd seen them there. I know Gretchen. I know how she thinks. She wouldn't go to Mexico. Anyway, I'm the one who taught her how to run away, as much as I hate to say it, and so I know."

"You taught her?" Battaglia asked.

"Yeah. Gretchen was going to run away one other time," he explained, "and she asked me how to do it. So I told her. I told her, whatever she did, not to go down into Mexico because down there she'd stand out like a sore thumb. I told her to either go to California, or to some big city, to fix herself up, and make herself look older."

"What about Wendy? Would she take her sister with her if she was going to run away?"

Gretchen's car discovered at the Flamingo Hotel in Tucson / Tucson Police Department

"Possibly," Smitty said. "Wendy was always with Gretchen, most every place she went. She's only thirteen, but she could make herself look a lot older if she wanted. Her and Gretchen

Gretchen's purse found inside of her car / Tucson Police Department

are identical in the way they think because they're almost always together. Yeah, I think Gretchen would take Wendy along."

"What about when they found her car at The Flamingo Hotel parking lot?" Bonanno inquired. "They also found her purse with her money in it."

"Oh that," Smitty said, laughing. "I told her to do that. That's just to throw the cops off the track."

"Did she usually have a lot of money with her?"

"Always. Or if she didn't, she could always get it."

"And you think she's in San Diego with this boyfriend?" Battaglia asked.

"Yes. I do," Smitty said, "I'm almost positive of it."

I was feeling as though I were in quicksand, unable to fight my way out, too confused and scared to think my way out, sinking deeper and deeper toward some dark ending. I had done nothing, but still I felt so much a part of his crimes only because I knew.

Would I eventually find proof and then talk, become a finger man and face being avenged by his friends? I would have to expect that, and fear it, if ever I did turn him in. Or would I stay quiet and continue to let it eat away at me and destroy me as it had already begun to? Would I continue to run the streets like a maniac only to hasten that ending?

From the time he had told me of how he raped, murdered, and buried Alleen Rowe, it had begun. And ever since Gretchen had come onto the scene, there had been a steady building of tempo, until now, the climax, when Gretchen too was dead. Now there was this with the Mafia, and I was there, right along with him, to face whatever consequences there were. I counted myself among his victims.

Momentarily, the voices in the room faded into the background. As Smitty and Battaglia continued to talk, I began to recall much of Gretchen's and Smitty's stormy and fatal romance—from the time they'd first seen each other, until the night he snuffed out the last living breath from her and left her lifeless form in some far-off remote place.

I remembered when they first met at a park swimming pool in August 1964. It was now late August 1965, and Gretchen and Wendy had been dead two weeks. Alleen had been dead since May 31, 1964, just three months prior to his and Gretchen's meeting.

Gretchen and Smitty had become romantic from the outset. Smitty had been attracted to her simply because she was a skinny, platinum blonde—he was notoriously crazy over skinny, platinum blondes—who seemed a bit scatter-brained to him. He had once described her as looking like a wreck waiting to happen. Gretchen had been attracted to him simply because he was fun-loving, mysterious Smitty, who so many of the girls in town described as the handsomest and sexiest guy around.

They looked good together—Smitty with his jet black hair and Gretchen with her blonde. They were both children of rich parents. Gretchen's father, a physician, was considered by many to be one of the world's leading heart surgeons.

At first, everything had been fine between them. They seemed made for each other. Then, suddenly, things changed for the worst. Gretchen began to dominate Smitty, dictating his every move. He had to be home at such and such a time every night to answer the phone, he couldn't go anywhere without her, he had to stop smoking, he had to stop drinking, he had to go to bed at this time, he had to call her at that, and he could have no friends, particularly no friends such as myself—she utterly detested me—and Paul G., his best friend since early childhood.

Heated arguments arose between them, but Gretchen always came out the victor. Smitty disguised and guarded his actions from her, seemingly terrified of what would happen if she discovered him doing anything contrary to her whims and wishes. I'd watched, dumbfounded over what was taking place, and after a while asked him why he put up with it.

"I took her out and showed her the body of Alleen," he told me. "I wanted her to see what kind of a person I was, to see if she really loved me. She told me she'd love me no matter what I did. Now she's blackmailing me with it. If I don't do exactly what she says, she'll go to the cops. You know what else she told me?" He asked.

"What?" I said.

"She said, 'You've had fun all of your life and I've been miserable. Now it's my turn to have fun and you're turn to be miserable.' I'm going to ring her neck!"

Yet, it was obvious he still loved her, in his own way, regardless of it. He wanted to own her, possess her, and he was filled with jealousy, suspicious of every instant he wasn't with her. He was convinced she was playing around on him. He watched her house almost as much as I now watched Kathy's. When he discovered her gone a few times when she wasn't supposed to be, he sent anonymous typewritten letters to her parents informing them that she was sneaking away and seeing him while they were out, contrary to their instructions that Gretchen was forbidden to see him.

When that hadn't kept her at home and away from the boys he'd imagined her seeing, he wrote an anonymous letter to the county health department, in which he stated she had gonorrhea and requested them to examine her. He even talked of throwing acid in her face, rationalizing that if she looked like a monster nobody would want her, and he had devised an ingenious plan to carry out the idea. The only catch was that he was afraid she'd be so ugly that he wouldn't want her either.

They fought, cursed each other's names, slapped each other back and forth in the middle of the street, and yelled so loud that the police had to be called in to quiet them down. They wrote on each other's cars with paint and lipstick, punctured each other's tires, spied upon each other endlessly, and accused each other of every wrongdoing in the book.

Gretchen had caught him with other girls, and, to humiliate him, made him insult them and tell them he never wanted to see their ugly faces again. Once, when she found him flirting, she even chased him up into a tree. She never stopped badgering him, screaming at him, and tormenting him for one second. Ugly rumors began to spread, affecting both Smitty and me, and when we checked them back, we found that Gretchen had been the source that triggered them.

"I hate her. I hate that bitch!" A hundred times a day he said it.

"Why don't you leave her then?" I would ask.

"Because I don't deserve any better than her, I guess. Maybe she's my punishment."

The Mafia

We'd be in his bedroom and the phone would ring. Wearily, he'd answer it. He'd talk softly to her for a few moments and then hold the receiver up in the air so that I, lounging on the bed on the other side of the room, could hear her screaming despite my distance from the phone.

"Why don't you just go to Hell?" he'd tell her and hang up. The phone would be ringing again almost instantly. He'd pick it up, yell something to her, and slam it back down again. He'd take the receiver off of the hook and go into the bathroom to comb his hair. He spent hours combing his hair. After a while, he'd return and summon me.

"Come on."

"Where we going?"

"To Gretchen's. I've had it with her this time. If she hates me so much, she can just go to the damned cops."

He'd storm from the house and I'd follow after. He'd speed through the streets toward her house, cruise past the house to make sure her car was in the driveway as it should be, and then drive to a phone booth to call her and arrange a meeting place. They'd meet, argue, talk, kiss, and he'd return smiling. But then the screaming and yelling would start all over again.

"I wish I had an excuse to break up with her," he'd say. "I can't take too much more, you know? She'd better cool it if she knows what's good for her."

Not long before she disappeared, Gretchen ran away from home to marry Smitty. They had gone away together one other time to Mexico to get married, but that time Gretchen had been unable to prove that she was eighteen years old and so they had been refused a license. This time she hid at Smitty's house.

I, a Squealer

"I pulled out the bottom drawer of my dresser," Smitty told me, "took the bottom off of it, and hid her in there. She actually had all the room from the floor to the second drawer to lay, but when I put the bottom drawer back in, nobody in the world could have guessed she was in there. Her mother called my mother, and my mother came over to search for her.

"While I had her in there," he confided to me, "I started thinking. Here she was, and she could be mine forever. That's what I thought I always wanted, but it wasn't until then that I realized I couldn't live with her forever. I didn't want her that way. I just wanted her as something to keep on the hook for whenever I felt like I needed her. I loved her, and I had to have her for my own, but not to marry her. I couldn't go through with it is all."

It was a couple of weeks later that he finally found his excuse to end his turmoil. Except that it went much further. That was on the night she returned from her vacation to California.

It was on the evening of August 16. There was a gathering of people at his house, and he was entertaining them when the phone rang. Someone picked it up and announced it was Gretchen. He talked with her for a bit, became enraged, and slammed the phone down. According to court testimony, he went into his bedroom, got a mysterious black satchel that some people later speculated contained a diary detailing the account of a fourth murder, tucked the satchel under his arm, and then left the house accompanied by Paul G., interestingly enough, "To go meet Gretchen." She was never seen alive again after that.

There was possibly something Gretchen could have said or

done in the last few seconds before she died that could have saved her life, but then she probably didn't. She had played the dominating roll for too long, and she paid dearly for it. Whether it was because she was threatening him, or because he was afraid of losing her, or because he was afraid to have her, or all three, or maybe he had just plain reached the point where he couldn't go on any longer, he killed her and ended it. But it was not over. It had only begun.

Bonanno turned to me and spoke my name, interrupting my thoughts, "You guys aren't planning on leaving town for any reason in the near future, are you?" he asked. "We'll probably be wanting to talk to you again, and so we'd like to know where we can find you if we come looking. You'll be around, won't you?"

"We'll be around," Smitty said. "You can always find me at my house there. If not, you can always find out where I am through my parents. They're in the house right next door."

"What about you Richard?"

"I'll be around," I said.

"We can find Richard through Smitty here, can't we?" Battaglia suggested.

"I don't know," Bonanno said. He looked at Smitty, "Do you know how to find Richard when you need him?"

"I've always been able to so far."

"That'd save us from having to come around to your house to look for you," Bonanno told me. "You're still living with your folks, aren't you?"

"Yes."

"Yeah, I think that'd be a better arrangement. Whenever we need you, we'll just get in touch with you through Smitty here."

I, a Squealer

He turned his attention back to Smitty. "Now tomorrow, Smitty, we want you to stay close to home the whole day. We might want to take you over to California to look for the girls, and so we want you to be ready for us, in case. All right?"

There was a delayed answer from across the room. "Take me to California?"

"Yeah. Don't you want to help find the girls, get them back home safe? I'm sure you're concerned and worried about them."

"Yes." he was visibly shaken. He hadn't anticipated this. They were really going to go through with it. They were going to call his bluff after all and take him to California!

"You told us you'd like to go over and look for them if you had a way to."

"Yes. Of course I want to go. More than anything in the world I want to go. I just didn't think you'd take me is all."

It was in moments like this that he was at his very best—when he was shaken and being tested. He was well rehearsed for such instances.

"I'll do anything to find them. I'm going crazy worrying over them. All I want is to get them back home safe. Man, I love Gretchen!" He put on one of his boyish expressions and continued, "I just want you to promise me one thing, though. If they turn up harmed in any way, I want you to promise me that you'll help me get whoever's responsible."

"We'd be happy to," Battaglia told him. "We'd be happy to."

Joe Jr. was now standing in the doorway waiting for us, and after Battaglia instructed him to drive us wherever we wanted to go, we left with him. I glanced back on the way out and saw the old man on the bed still playing with his hands and staring at Bonanno's chair.

"We'll see ya," Bonanno said.

"Yeah…we'll see ya," Smitty replied.

Joe's partner joined us outside, and the four of us walked together to the car. In the car and cruising down Speedway again, Smitty started to talk with Joe. "You guys really are sincere about trying to find Gretchen and Wendy, aren't you?" he asked.

"Yeah, we're sincere," Joe replied. "Why? You think we're going to all of this trouble because we're not?"

"No, I just didn't want to get any false hopes up is all."

"We'll find them; don't worry. You told these guys tonight everything you know, didn't you?"

"Everything we know, yes."

"I hope so, for your sake anyway. You know, you're lucky these men only talk. When the other guys get into it they do a lot more than just talk, you know? So if you do know something that you haven't told us yet, now's the time to tell, before the other guys do get into it."

Other guys. What other guys? They do a lot more than just talk. That struck home with both of us.

Instead of returning to his house again, we had Joe and his associate drive us to Johnnie's Drive-In, a restaurant on Speedway and one of the bigger teen hangouts in town. They dropped us off there and left.

"What are we going to do?" I asked after they had gone.

"I don't know," he answered. "It looks like she's going to win after all, Richie. She's going to come back and beat me anyway. All the way from the grave. You did it, Gretchen. You actually, finally did it, didn't you?"

I, a Squealer

"Well, what are we going to do?" I persisted.

"What can we do?"

"What are you going to do if they take you over to California? What are you going to do over there?"

"Fake it out as best I can, I guess. It's all I can do. What I'm worried about is if the bodies are found. I didn't even bury them, you know."

"You didn't even bury them!"

"No. They're just laying out on the side of a hill, right in plain view of anyone who happens to stumble across them. I don't know what the hell we're going to do," he added.

Suddenly I found I had to sit down somewhere. We sat on a wall and watched the kids circling the drive-in in their cars, rumbling about and checking each other over as we meditated on our new predicament. My mind was a complete blank, but Smitty's evidently became inspired.

Several hours and several beers later, back at his house once more, he did the most unlikely thing imaginable. He got on the phone and called the FBI. First he called the local branch, but there was no answer. He called the FBI in Phoenix. Still no help. He put in a person-to-person call to J. Edgar Hoover in Washington. It would have been around two o'clock in the morning in Washington. Of course, Mr. Hoover wasn't in his office. Someone did take the call, however, and promised to have an agent get in touch with him by late morning.

"That might be too late. These guys are coming for me, and they might come before then. I need someone right away. I need protection!"

"Well, we don't offer protection," the man told him.

"But I need protection!" He screamed frantically. "I can't fight 'em all by myself. If they take me over to California, it's hard to tell what they might do to me there. If you guys won't help when the Mafia screws with somebody, then who the hell will?"

Who had helped Gretchen? I thought. And who'd helped Wendy and Alleen? They were beyond help now. They were dead. I'd envisioned each one a thousand times over, and so I knew. No one had helped them. But Kathy was still alive and could be helped, and I would always be there to protect her. I would protect her because I was being driven by an insane dream.

"I didn't say we wouldn't help you," the man went on. "Now what's your name and address?"

"Charles Schmid, 422 East Adams Street, Tucson, Arizona."

"Okay, we'll have someone in touch with you soon."

"Please hurry."

Yes, I was being driven by a dream. A dream, but nothing more. Could I distinguish it from reality? Would I ever be able to? I had never once doubted my dream, and so to me it was reality. But it was fantasy, and it remained fantasy. It had been, from the start, nothing but fantasy—exaggerating and changing with each repetition of itself. Endless fantasy, wild and uncontrollable, running amok, driving me on and on forever. There had to come a time to face it, to acknowledge it for what it really was, and to search out and find the real truth.

What I did next I had to do. If there were bodies I had to see them. It was a calculated risk, but now was the time. He was ready for it. The next move was mine, and I made it.

I, a Squealer

"Look," I said, "my neck's in this now too. If you didn't bury those bodies, I'm not going to take the chance of them being found. Let's go bury them."

4

Columbus, Ohio

From Broad Street to State Street the sidewalks were buried beneath rain-soaked leaves. They gave way under my feet as I walked, cushioning my steps and absorbing my weight to make it seem as though I were walking on air. Overhead, trickles of rain water traveled down branches, reaching a point where they would stop, grow into drops, hang until they could hang on no longer, and then fall to meet me as I passed below.

Far overhead, rumbles of thunder filled the air and then reverberated along the avenue—off the rooftops, off the black pavement of the street where a car splashed noisily by, and off the puddles that reflected the gray, overcast sky. The clouds, like smoke, took on weird and eerie shapes as they moved with the wind. Otherwise it was quiet. Too quiet.

Already I ached for home, but I had not yet felt the urgency or magnitude of my situation. That would come later, after the numbness of how I'd come to be there had worn off.

"It is the order of this court, Richard, that you be placed on one year's probation, conditions of which are as follows: One, you are not to have any contact with any member of Kathy's family whatsoever, in any manner whatsoever, and you are to remain off of Kathy's street. You are not to enter any alleys that intersect her street, or to walk down the drive of any thoroughfares that intersect her street. You are not to enter any alleys that are closer than a block to her street or house. Two, you are to leave the state of Arizona for a period of not less than six months to go live with your grandmother in Columbus, Ohio, and you are not to re-enter the state at any time during that period, for any reason, without the knowledge and permission of this court."

So I boarded a plane, and watched Tucson grow miniature in size and soon disappear. I had flown over two thousand miles above a sea of clouds, into my past, to the place where I was born.

This was a green place. Everything was so green. Trees everywhere—big, beautiful green trees with an intoxicating fragrance brought alive by the recent rain, and beautiful green grass was on every lawn. This was not the wiry brown stuff of the type I'd seen for the past ten years, but velvety green grass—the kind you could lie down and go to sleep on.

Everywhere I looked it was green and beautiful, but my eyes were blinded to it. It was foreign and strange to me. I didn't belong there, and it was frightening. I yearned for the dry air, the bright sun, and the baked dust. I yearned for the prickly weeds, and the giant saguaro cactus that hulk against the sky and paint such a panoramic picture when silhouetted against the mountains and the great western sunset.

I wanted to be back home in the wide open spaces where a person could find solitude. I wanted to be back where things were new and modern, and not old as they were here—the people and the two story houses with pointed roofs and attics, and basements with coal furnaces. This all seemed rather gloomy to me.

As I strolled along, the buildings and streets only looked remotely familiar. I couldn't remember them, except for maybe the house where I had lived as a kid, but it was the feeling inside that I remembered—that spooky, ghastly feeling that made my blood run cold.

Whenever I remembered my childhood there, I always remembered myself as a boy confined in the dark corridors of an isolated, prison-like school that reeked with the smell of wet clothes, of standing in front of an ark-shaped window listening to the echoes of the hall and staring into the miserable gray outside, of listening to the thunder and watching the rain hit the ground.

I remembered passing through a 15-foot high steel gate to get to my school bus, and of driving out onto a country road, and there looking back at the school for the last time— a bleak scene of one faded brick building, in a corner all by itself, standing as a monument to what I was leaving behind: the depressing and the old.

I felt no different now than I had then, except that now I was older, and with ties, urgent ties a great distance away. Now I could not leave, but I had to leave. Now the world was darker than ever. The clouds only accented what had already become a part of me.

"Did you enjoy your walk?" My grandmother asked as I walked through the door. "I'll bet you didn't remember too much of it. You were probably too young."

"I remembered it a little bit," I said. "It sure is dark outside. I'm so used to the sun."

"Well, it'll be starting to get colder now—November already. Probably snow before long."

Snow. How long it had been since I'd seen snow! Something good was cooking in the kitchen. I smelled it as soon as I walked in. "What's for dinner?" I asked.

"Chicken and mashed potatoes. I'm just now getting ready to put it on the table, so you'd better run up and get washed if you want to eat."

Ah, chicken and mashed potatoes. My favorite. I walked up the stairs to the bathroom, washed my hands, and then descended the stairs as she was preparing the table. I sat and watched her as she brought the chicken from the stove and placed it on a plate in front of me.

"Do you still make them doughnuts you used to make?" I asked. I remembered her doughnuts more than anything. I always loved her homemade doughnuts.

"Oh goodness. It's been ages since I made those. You still remember Gram's doughnuts?"

"Couldn't forget 'em."

"Well then, I'll just have to get busy and make you some soon. How's that?"

"That's fine with me," I said laughing.

We started to eat, and by the time we had finished it was totally dark outside. I got up from the table and walked out to the living room, where I flicked on the television set and plopped down in my grandfather's old easy chair. My grandfather wasn't there. He'd passed away several years back.

"They still have the fights on TV here?" I asked. My grandfather had never missed the fights when he'd been around.

"I don't know if they still have them on or not. I haven't seen fights for so long. Maybe they don't show 'em anymore. I couldn't say, though. I don't like fights."

I sat for a while and then returned to the kitchen where my grandmother was washing dishes. From the refrigerator I got some of the beer that I'd bought the night before and went back out to the living room. I downed the beer and returned for more.

Throughout the evening I continued to go back for more beer until it was all gone. I then went to bed to try to get some sleep—to prayerfully forget.

Maybe my nightmare hadn't followed me.

5

Finding Gretchen and Wendy

I visualized it all so well as I lay there. It was worse than any nightmare, and I re-lived it again—every traumatic, macabre moment.

Two headlights were beaming through the night, making their way along a narrow desert path—dodging and weaving, dipping, leveling, rising toward the sky, and then leveling again, changing direction as the road changed direction—constantly changing direction, until they finally stopped at the top of a hill and died out. They were followed by one faint light that lit up and revealed the interior of a car with two men inside. One was getting out—the passenger, and then the driver was getting out. Slam, slam, and the light was gone.

"I dumped them in the most obvious place." This was what he meant. Our old drinking spot, where between us we had downed a ton of booze and brought countless scores of people. We had thrown numerous parties there, and it was where we had brought our girlfriends on dates. It was our own private Lover's Lane above the city lights, where each of us had come whenever we wanted to be alone. I hadn't believed it. For the first time, for just one moment I'd doubted my dream. Perhaps he'd been stalling. Perhaps there had been no bodies at all, and I was close to ending my dream forever.

"Get the shovel."

I walked to the rear of the car and took out the shovel we brought. Together we started to descend the hill from the road.

"They're down here about a couple hundred yards," he said. We walked that distance in the dark. "They're around here someplace. Start looking. They can't be far. Wait a minute. I smell something."

I took a breath and smelled something also. It smelled like something dead and rotting.

"You go over that way," he said pointing, "and I'll go over this way. They've got to be around here somewhere."

In robot fashion I did as I was told. He went straight, and I went off to the left. I moved slowly, my eyes fixed to the ground. Every shadow I saw was a body to me. The smell seemed to be getting closer and closer. It grew stronger with every step I took. It was such an overpowering, sickening smell.

My foot kicked something solid; I was almost afraid to look. It was so damned dark out I could hardly see. I must have been right where the smell was coming from; it was so strong. I glared through the darkness at what was at my feet. I knelt down, reached out with my hand, and my fingers touched something. My hand pulled back with lightening speed, as though it were a rattlesnake I was trying to touch. It was a dead barrel cactus.

"Over here," he called.

I rose to my feet. He couldn't be that far off. I started to move in the direction of his voice, but stopped in my tracks. I had a premonition, a frightful premonition, that I could be walking to my death. He might kill me. Of course. Why shouldn't he kill me? I knew too much. Maybe that was why he'd agreed to bring me there, to kill me.

I thought of running, but then he'd kill me for sure. Besides, where could I run to? He knew where I lived. He knew how to find me. He'd have to kill me if I ran because then he'd know he couldn't trust me. I had to make him think that he could trust me. I had to make him think that I was just like him.

I had to go to him to see what I had come to see, to know that I wasn't going through hell for nothing. I took one step, and then another. I moved cautiously, slowly. As I left that spot I left the greater part of myself behind with it.

At first I couldn't find him anywhere. I pushed the branch of an oversized mesquite out of my way and pricked my finger on one of its thorns.

"Where in the hell are you?"

"I'm right here," he said softly.

I turned and looked down. He was no more than twenty feet away, kneeling over something on the ground. I approached him.

"That's Gretchen," he whispered and nodded toward a patch of dark earth in front of him.

At my feet now was a coal black object, indistinguishable in form, in the center of what appeared to be burnt earth. I looked down at it from where I was standing. It looked like the site of a campfire, or where dirty oil had been spilt over a log and allowed to soak into the ground. My God! This thing couldn't be human! Damn, it was dark out! I couldn't make out anything. I knelt for a better look.

There was one large spot of white in the center of it. I studied it to determine what it was. It looked like a brassiere, the kind that extends over the full length of the midriff. My eyes continued in line with it until they came upon something else. It looked like a pair of legs dressed in Capri pants. I followed them down. At the ankles was tied a white rag, knotted in the center, binding the two legs together. From there, my eyes moved back up the form again.

I touched the brassiere. I could feel it. It was real! I looked to where the head should be. Nothing but black. I reached out for it. My fingers touched something coarse and wiry. I placed my whole hand on it. It felt liked stiffened hair. I pulled my hand away. My stomach churned.

"Wendy should be up that way," he said, glancing up the incline of the hill. He rose to his feet and started to ascend the hill that ran parallel with the road—a different one than the one we'd come down in the beginning—and I followed after, about twenty steps back. He stopped abruptly and pointed to a bush across from him. I drew closer.

"That's Wendy," he said.

I looked to where he was pointing. Next to the bush was a mound of black dirt. We walked up to it. I looked, hunched over it, and looked again closely. Something was protruding out of the top of it. Dear Lord, it was a foot with a girl's shoe on it, and part of a leg.

"I wanted to at least cover her up," he said.

Now we stood in silence, as one would stand in silence

and appraise irreparable damage. I was so horror-stricken I couldn't even think. I was too stunned to even feel emotion. The gruesomeness, the brazenness of it was impossible for me to grasp right away. It was too horrible a sight to accept as the reality I had come in search of. Nothing real could be so awful as this. In my wildest of nightmares I had never envisioned it like this. I wanted to believe, even now, that it was only a part of my nightmare. But I knew it wasn't. This was the culmination of my dream, but what my dream could never have portrayed so vividly. I wondered if he felt pride over it—standing there, showing me his handiwork.

We walked down to the bottom of the hill into the dry wash, and we tried to dig. First I tried to dig, and then he tried, but the ground was too hard and we couldn't dig in it with the shovel we had. The shovel was the kind used for scooping. It was flat on the end and didn't have a point.

"We ain't going to get anywhere in this stuff," I yelled to him. He was off searching for softer ground to dig in. I wanted to get out of there, to get away safe, to try to forget what I had seen. I couldn't live with the constant memory of it, I knew that. I tried to take my mind off of it and off of the danger I was in, but it was no good. He returned in a minute.

"The ground's like this all over," he said when he came back into view.

"Well, it's like rock here. We'll never be able to dig a grave in this. Not with this shovel anyway."

"I wonder what time it is."

"I don't know, but it's late. I know that much."

He looked around him, to appraise the situation, while he

thought.

"It'll probably be starting to get light soon," I coaxed. "I'd hate to be caught out here in the daylight."

"Well, we can't leave them laying out there like that. At least not Gretchen. She's right out there in the open, you know? Wendy's at least covered up." He paused and thought a second longer. "Come on."

He walked back up to where Gretchen was laying and I followed him up. He grabbed her by the rag tied around her ankles and started dragging her down into the wash. It made a sound like dragging a hollow shell across the ground. I watched him, and after he'd dragged her off the black ground she was on and out into the open, I could see her whole body. Her right arm was up over her head, and her left arm was down at her side. She had her blouse open. I followed him down the hill.

He dragged the body to the wash, and then down the wash, and dumped it under a clump of bush. He left it there, and started up the hill again. He passed me, then stopped and turned back.

"I might have left some fingerprints on her shoes. Go down and wipe them off."

"Wipe them off?"

"Yes. Wipe them off." His body stiffened when he said it. His eyelids narrowed, and he peered at me intensely through them, waiting for my reaction.

I hesitated. I tried to speak out, but I stopped myself. He was testing me. I had to prove myself to him, and if I failed, he would kill me. Hesitating or speaking out would be fatal.

I went down to where she lay in the wash. I took my

Finding Gretchen and Wendy

handkerchief out of my back pocket, wiped over her shoes with it, and, not wanting to place it back into my pocket, tossed it away. When I came back out again, he was walking back up toward Wendy. I followed him up the hill. When I got there he said, "Take off her shoe and throw it." I grabbed her shoe, slipped it off—it came right off—and threw it. Then he told me, "You're in this as deep as I am now." From there, we walked back up to the car, put the shovel in the trunk, and drove off.

———————— o ————————

I heard the refrigerator door slam downstairs. I threw the covers off of me, sat up on the edge of the bed, and looked about the room. I'd forgotten where I was. I broke out into a cold sweat as I glanced around. The room seemed to swirl; the walls seemed to close in around me. Then I knew.

Kathy! Where was Kathy? I had to find her. I had to tell her Smitty was coming for her, and that she was in danger. He was coming to take her out to the desert, to make her do all of those things he'd made Alleen do—just like in my dream—and then kill her.

He would kill her! I had to find her to help her. I had to protect her. But where was she? Oh God, that was it! That was why I could never get to her in my dream. I was too far away. He was already with her. They were already out in the desert. Maybe she was already dead!

I jumped up from the bed and ran to the window. I looked out at the wooden houses across the street: strange houses, with porches and steps leading up to the porches, and with attics, and gabled roofs. The street there—it would go on and on and

57

never find its way to her. She was no longer just down the block. She was a million miles away from me, and she was only seven miles away from Smitty. He could have covered that distance in minutes, and the desert was only a little ways further.

How could I know? There was no way. She had exiled me from her. Why? Hadn't she known? Oh, why hadn't I told her? Why was it that every time I picked up the phone to call her I would put it down again just before I dialed the last number? Why hadn't I blurted it out in court, in front of her parents and everybody? Why hadn't I told the FBI men who had been waiting for us when we'd gotten back from the bodies that night? They'd asked me, and Smitty had been in the other room, but I told them I didn't know where Gretchen and Wendy were. Why had I been afraid? Why was I afraid to go downstairs to the phone now and call?

No! It was too big a thing. I couldn't start it. If I told, I would be a finger man, and everyone would hate me. Just think of all I would start if I called. I might even get put into prison. After all, it had already been two months since the time I'd been out to the bodies with Smitty. That's a long time to hold on to information. They'd kill me in prison because I'd talked.

If I called, I would be betraying a friend. Think of what I'd be doing to him! I held his very life in the balance. And I couldn't hate him. I was deeply attached to him in spite of everything. I actually pitied him, even though I feared him so much. How would he look at me if I turned him in? I'd have to face him. Could I face him? Could I face anyone? Could I face his friends? He had so many friends. The whole town knew him. He was like a legend there.

Finding Gretchen and Wendy

But Kathy. *What about you? Oh, Kathy, it's too late! God knows I tried, but it's too late.* Tears welled in my eyes. She was so helpless against him. Was there any stopping him? He would go on and on. He had to be stopped. But I just couldn't do it. *I've got to do it. Everything is moving so fast. Damn.*

I fell back onto the bed. I rolled over and stared at the door. As a small boy I'd lain in that bed. I remembered the times, beneath the covers, peaking out at the door. I'd lay there waiting for the moment when I could build up enough courage to break for the door and run downstairs before the ghouls could get me. *Downstairs. I have to call. I have to. I can't go on. I can't!*

6

Blowing the Whistle

I never slept so well as I did the rest of that night. I hadn't slept long, but when I awoke early the following morning it was like I was waking up to a whole new world. I don't believe I had ever felt quite so rested or at ease as I did then. I woke up almost in a type of excitement, in anticipation of something wonderful.

"Richard," my grandmother said.

"Yes?"

"You'd better get up and start packing your things if you think those men will be here early."

"Okay Grandma." *Oh, they'll be here early, all right. You can bet on that.*

"What time is it?" I called out to her.

"It's after eight o'clock already."

"Okay. I'll be right down."

I dressed hurriedly, went into the bathroom at the opposite end of the hall to comb my hair, then went downstairs for breakfast.

I, a Squealer

She didn't say anything to me. I guess there wasn't much she could say. I sat there at the table and thought about what was going to happen. Like a wild gangster drama unfolding in my mind, I saw the whole sequence of events taking place.

For the moment, I couldn't feel for him. It was as though suddenly I didn't even know him. The pain was completely gone now, as if by some sort of instant magic, and it was such a relief. I was amazingly at ease, and it felt so good. But that feeling ended when the doorbell rang.

I was almost done packing. I went and opened the door.

"Richard Bruns?" asked one of the two men on the porch.

"Yes."

"Police." He held out an open wallet with a badge pinned inside of it. Then the other flashed his badge. "Sergeant Wilhelm, Tucson Police."

"Oh yeah, come on in."

They came in and watched me pack, and one of them asked me if I was about finished.

"Yes."

Then the other asked my grandmother if I'd told her anything about it.

"Just what he told me last night. I thought he was drunk."

When I was done with my packing they escorted me out to their car. I said goodbye to my grandmother. We waved to each other as she stood on the porch and watched me leave with the officers.

I spent the rest of the day at police headquarters in downtown Columbus. There I gave statements and signed papers. I agreed to go back with Sergeant Wilhelm to help locate the bodies.

Blowing the Whistle

"Why didn't you come out with all of this sooner?" he asked.

"I don't know. I tried to. Many times I tried. I just couldn't. I was afraid to."

"This is murder, though. This is mass murder! He's killed three, possibly four girls, and it's hard to tell where he'd stop."

"I know," I said. "That's why I finally turned him in. I couldn't go along with that, not that."

It was a long day, but at five o'clock we were at the airport, and soon we were on a plane on our way back to Tucson. The trip was long. At O'Hare Airport in Chicago we were held over for hours because of the blackout that took place on the east coast that night (November 9th, 1965), and when they finally did re-route a plane and we boarded, it was another two hours before we landed at home.

At the airport in Tucson we were met by four other policemen. We picked up my baggage, and in one car we drove to a private lodge in town, where they had rented three rooms for us to stay. Of course, I got the middle room with a private guard, and they surrounded me on both sides.

"Tomorrow, bright and early, we go out and find Gretchen and Wendy," the lieutenant announced. "So you better get some sleep. It'll be an even longer day tomorrow."

"I don't feel like sleeping," I said. "I think I'll just stay awake and talk."

At dawn it began. We went to a restaurant for breakfast, and there the detectives started to accumulate, coming in individually about every five minutes until two tables were filled.

"Everybody ready?" the lieutenant asked.

I, a Squealer

Richard and detectives on the way to grave site / Tucson Police Department

Pontatoc Road in Tucson / Tucson Police Department

Blowing the Whistle

Dirt Road off of Pontatoc Road leading to grave site / Tucson Police Department

Dirt Road off of Pontatoc Road leading to grave site / Tucson Police Department

I, a Squealer

"We're all ready if Richard here is."

They were all looking toward me.

"I'm ready. As ready as I'll ever be."

"Okay. Let's go."

I rode in the lead car and pointed the way. We drove north, past the city limits, and into the foothills for half a mile before I could see the dirt road leading to the grave site.

"That's the road we'll have to take up there," I said, pointing.

"All right."

The car fought its way up over the rough, jagged stones, and through the holes and pits. The car would lean and then straighten, the driver would give it the gas for some other obstacle, until finally we were at the crest of the hill.

"There's a sharp turn to the right here," I warned.

He turned the wheel, and then we were pointed toward the old drinking spot. This part of the road was full of dips and turns, but in the daylight it didn't seem nearly as treacherous as it did at night. We rounded a turn, the car sank into the dip on the other side, and then rose again.

"Stop at the top. This is it," I said.

The other car following us pulled up behind. Everyone got out.

"You'll have to help me look," I instructed. "They're down here about a couple hundred yards; I'd say in a square about— oh, I'd say fifty yards that way, and a hundred and fifty that way. They're just laying out on the ground, so you'll be able to see them."

"Okay. Men, spread out," the lieutenant commanded. The policemen spread out and started down the hill about ten yards apart from each other. I walked straight down from the car, the way I'd remembered Smitty had done.

Minutes passed. Nothing. I looked around me at the men combing the hillside, all with their eyes fixed on the ground, kicking bushes and occasionally a beer can out of the way, but finding nothing.

I tried to fix my direction according to the car, but I thought I was where I should be. Gretchen should have been right there, but she wasn't. Wendy should have been somewhere up there, where those men were. Why weren't any of them yelling they'd found something? Oh, God.

On the plane it had occurred to me, and I'd thought and worried about it all night—what if he'd moved the bodies? What if they weren't there? Or, worse yet, what if they never had been there? I'd never allowed myself to fully believe they had. Somehow, deep down, I'd forbidden myself to. It had occurred to me many times that perhaps I was insane. Maybe I'd invented the whole thing because of my nightmare.

No. It was real. *Damn it! They have to be around here somewhere.* I started searching frantically, almost running. I gasped.

I stopped and stood there alone, looking down. One by one the detectives came and stood beside me.

"Which one's that?"

"That's Gretchen," I whispered.

Sergeant Wilhelm came. The lieutenant turned to him.

"Could that be?"

"I don't know. It don't take long for something to decompose out here. It's been a couple of months already."

I, a Squealer

"What color was her hair?"

"That color."

The faces were grim. At our feet was a human skull, human hair, and human bones scattered over a large area. A photographer began to snap pictures.

"It looks like animals got to her," the lieutenant said. He studied the remains.

"I don't know. Are you sure this isn't Wendy, Richard?" he asked. "It seems to me that this looks more like it would by Wendy than Gretchen, judging from the size of the skull, you know?"

"Well, if it is then Gretchen's down there. Yeah. Yeah, I think it is Wendy. I got my directions fouled up. Gretchen's down that way."

Just as he'd left her that night, Gretchen was in the wash under the clump of bush. Bits of her clothes, unraveled and in shreds, clung to her skeletal remains. One of her legs had been torn off, evidently by an animal, and was above her head. She was more intact than Wendy; the clothes had been a discouragement to the animals. There were no clothes found with Wendy.

Strands of hair remained in the top of her skull, while the rest was on the ground around her body and hanging off the branches of bush. The brassiere I'd touched had turned brown. Dried mud from when it had rained was caked on parts of the bones. Ants and other insects were crawling over her body.

"Richard," the lieutenant called.

"Yeah."

He walked over to me.

Detectives at grave site of Gretchen and Wendy Fritz
Tucson Police Department

Richard and detectives at grave site of Gretchen and Wendy Fritz
Tucson Police Department

Blowing the Whistle

"We want this guy! Now, I know you've told us you don't think he'll confess, but when we do get him we want to hit him with everything we can to try to make him confess. I want to get the two of you together. I want you to face him. He might just confess if we hit him with enough. The more the cards look stacked against him, the more chance there is of him confessing. Will you do that?"

"Oh, man," I said, recoiling, "No! He won't confess, I can tell you that much. He'll just yell for his lawyer. I know there's nothing I can say to him. I'm just no match for him. He'll play it cool. He'll tear me apart."

"He might not play it as cool as you think. Not facing two murder charges. You don't have to say anything. I just want you there, for him to see, for him to know what we've got against him."

"I don't want to see him. I couldn't stand to see him. Not now."

7

Face to Face

"What'll you have, sir?"

I tossed my menu down onto the table and gave the waitress my order.

"Thank you. And you, sir?" she said, facing the detective that sat with me.

I watched people entering and leaving the restaurant, mostly business people on their lunch hour, as I crumpled cigarette after cigarette into the ashtray. I tapped my fingers on the table nervously, lit a cigarette, took a few drags off of it, and put it out. I was already on my fifth pack since the time I'd last slept. I was spending an eternity right there, waiting for word.

The waitress brought the food, I nibbled away at it and then pushed it aside. I couldn't eat. Not now. What was taking so long? I lit another cigarette. I put it out. I looked at the clock. In all that time its hands had hardly moved. A man pushed open the plate glass door to the place and entered. He looked the type. I watched him as he approached our table.

"Let's go," he said.

"Have you....?"

I, a Squealer

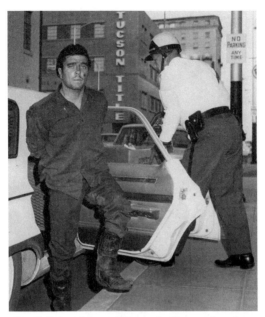

*Charles Schmid being led into the Tucson Courthouse
to be charged with murder*

John Kamman / Tucson Daily Citizen

"Yes, we've got him."

What happened from then until the time I was standing atop those concrete stairs leading to the basement of that building I can scarcely remember. We'd just driven through the streets of downtown, from the restaurant to there, and the cop had asked me if this guy had anything on me. I'd told him no.

What I felt during that time would be impossible to describe. It was anything but relief. I just kept praying, *don't make me do it. Please don't make me face him.* Now he was in the room down there (I could see the screened window to it from where I was standing), and they were making me go down there to him.

I called; they flew me back; I took them to the bodies and

showed them. Hadn't that been enough? What more could I do? Why were they making me do this? The men accompanying me were conferring with each other, and then one of them told me to "come on." I walked down the stairs and through the door at the bottom.

Inside, two men were standing in the hallway looking through a two-way mirror in the door leading to the room. I stopped, and listened. I could hear the faint sound of my voice: "It was around seven or so in the morning that the FBI men drove us back over to Smitty's house again."

"Richard."

"Huh?"

"You like to see him?" the man gestured with his hand, offering me his place at the mirror.

I started to move—a reflex, as though following a command —but held back. I didn't want to see him like an imprisoned animal, put on exhibition there to be stared and gawked at. I didn't want to see him that way. But I had to. I had to for the same reason I would go to see an auto accident and see people sprawled and splattered on the pavement. Except this was happening to me. This was the closing chapter of my own tragedy. Of course I had to go.

I went to the mirror. I walked up to it and turned my body toward it. But I kept my eyes on the cop. He was smiling now with deep satisfaction. Then I turned my head and looked in at Smitty.

He was sitting in a chair facing me, gazing off at the floor, listening to the finish of my tape recording: "The next day, these mafia guys came and picked him up, and took him over to California. His parents came over to my house right after to see if they'd taken me, too. Smitty told me they took him over there, and they were walking along the beach with Gretchen and Wendy's pictures, and that some guys ended up shooting at him, and that he and these mafia guys were picked up on suspicion of murdering Gretchen and Wendy but that he was released after the cops called here and found out there wasn't any proof against him."

Hearing myself on the recording, seeing him there listening to it, helped relieve me some. He was aware now that I was the one who had turned him in, and so when they made me go in to face—confront him, to make him confess, I could go in knowing that he was already expecting it and that I wouldn't have to be the one to tell him.

Mostly, it was a relief to know it was all over and couldn't be changed. There was nothing I could do, nothing I had to do. It was entirely out of my hands, and that felt good.

I was called away by a group of detectives who were huddling together close by, mapping out their strategy. I walked over to them. The chief of police was there, along with virtually every other high-ranking official on the force.

"Do you feel rested enough to take a lie detector test?"

"Yes, I guess so."

"Do you feel up to facing him?" the Lieutenant continued. "I still think that if we get the two of you together in a room, to further confront him with all of this, that he might just confess."

"I don't know…. I guess so. I don't know! I'm too nervous. I'm too shook."

"If you could just face him, that might be all he needs."

Face to Face

"Yes. Yes, I'll face him if you want me to."

One of the detectives left the group and went into the room with Smitty. I felt like letting go and screaming. I was perspiring all over. Directly overhead a large bulb was burning, flooding the dingy hallway with a yellow, murky kind of light. It was so hot in there. I was so tired. *Damn! No, I don't want to go in there and face him. I want to go home, anywhere out of here. What will I say? What will I do? I can't even think. My mind's in a damned maze. I'm too confused and tired. I don't want to go in there.*

The door to the room opened, and the detective who had just gone in held it open and motioned for me to come. I felt the blood rushing to my head. My head was so hot. The air in there was so thin I could hardly breath. My legs felt weak. They moved. Barely. Everyone was so much stronger than me. They commanded me. I didn't have the power to resist them. All I could think was that I would soon be out of there. I'd be out in the fresh air again when this was over, and that was all that

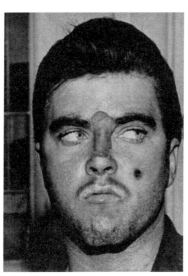

Charles Schmid / John Kamman / Tucson Daily Citizen

mattered. I turned the corner through the doorway and went in.

He looked up when I entered. At the sight of me his expression changed from one of almost total insouciance to one of utter hate. His lip curled, and the muscles in his face strained as he watched me walk to the chair straight across from him to sit down. One of his eyes was partially closed, while the other, wide and afire with the hate inside him, cut away at me as though I were a piece of raw meat, destroying my defenses, and drawing the warmth right out of my body. They were so sinister—his eyes—as if he were emanating the devil himself from them.

Even without the look in his eyes he was a frightening sight. I'd never seen him looking as bad as this. He was mean looking. His black hair was blown and messed, and part of it was hanging down over his forehead. His skin, from lack of care, was yellowed from the layers of makeup caked on it. The bandage was still on his nose, and the beauty mark was still there; it looked like a giant blotch of axle grease smudged on his cheek. He was unshaven and unbathed; I could smell him from where I was sitting. His shirt, worn and dirty and soaked with perspiration, was opened, baring his chest and the dyed hairs on it. His pants, only a slight bit blacker than his shirt, were stained and unpressed. The cuffs of them were tucked into his boots, which were bulging with the trash he'd wadded inside of them.

This was what, at one time, had been one of the most immaculate and clean persons I had known—a pretty boy, an idol, the teenager's hero, wild and cool Smitty, the parents' ideal. He had certainly come to the very pit of the gutter. He just sat there and stared at me.

Face to Face

The interrogation officer in the room clicked off the recorder. No one said anything. The cop looked over at me. To avoid Smitty's intensifying glare, I look away from him and toward the officer.

"I know why you did it," Smitty said at last.

"Did what?" I had to swallow a giant lump in my throat.

"Put the finger on me."

I wanted to try to plead with him, to make him understand. *Man, you're sick. Don't you know that? I had to. You're sick. You need help.*

"I know why you did it. I know."

"Know what?"

"It's not going to work," he said, smiling menacingly.

"What's not going to work?" the cop asked.

"He knows," Smitty went on, the smile growing larger.

"What's he talking about?" the cop asked me. "I thought you told us he didn't have anything on you."

"He don't. I don't know what he's talking about."

"You know. It was a nice try, Richie. Nice frame job."

"What?" I turned to the cop. "He's trying to make it seem like I did it!"

"Well, didn't you?" Smitty asked.

So that was it. I'd expected it. I'd known it, but I still couldn't help staring at him in disbelief. He was going to say that I did it, that I killed the girls. He'd planned it this way. I could only think that it had all been planned.

"You're not going to get away with it," he continued.

"I just....No," I answered, "No, you're not going to accuse me."

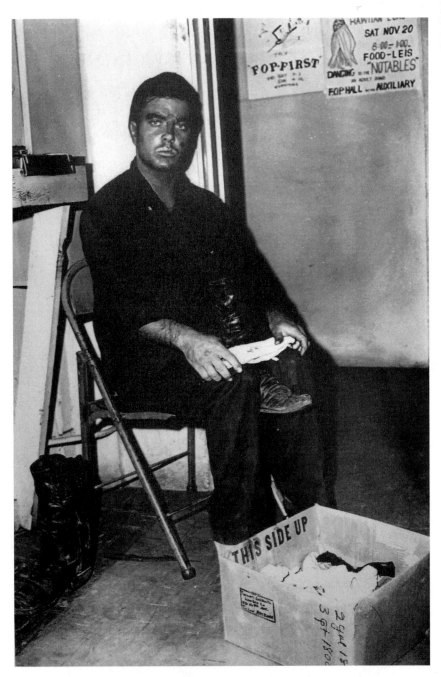

*Charles Schmid removing his boots and placing everything stuffed
inside of his boots into a box / Tucson Police Department*

Face to Face

All of the rags and miscellaneous items that were stuffed inside Schmid's boots
Tucson Police Department

I could see that he was trying to defend himself in the only way he could, by pointing the finger of guilt right back at me, his accuser. I was the one he had once trusted but who now sat before him with a single, most damning objective in mind. I was the friend who had just become the most dangerous and hated person in his life. For the moment I had been put on the defensive, and with all the tortures I had suffered because of him, locked somewhere inside of me but now being forced out, I was fighting back. I no longer feared him. In fact, sitting there in that chair, looking at him staring me down that way, I found myself surprisingly unaffected by him. To the contrary, in that moment he even seemed trivial and harmless.

"The crap I've gone through for you," I said, half through my teeth, and with a stare equal to his own, "because of you. All because of you. You bastard."

"You'll pay. It'll all come out in court. I'll prove my innocence at my trial."

"You may not know it," the cop chided, "but you may have to stand trial four times."

He tried to answer but failed. There were no words. The viciousness drained from his eyes, and alarm showed in its place. "I want to see my lawyer," he said.

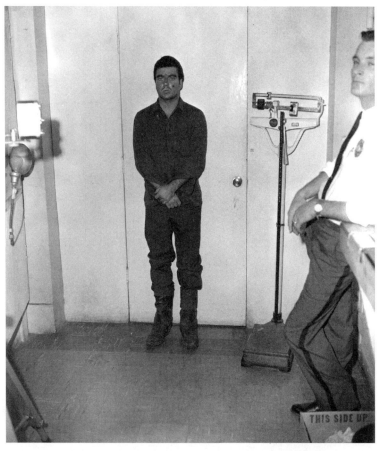

Photograph taken of Schmid at the time he was booked for the murders of Gretchen and Wendy Fritz / Tucson Police Department

8

Leaving

On Monday, June 26, 1967, I was preparing to hitchhike to Phoenix, one hundred and thirty miles to the north of Tucson, to look for work.

I was leaving town because I had to leave. I could no longer stay in Tucson, especially with the events of the last couple of weeks still so vividly etched on the people's minds there.

The fire from Smitty's first trial over a year ago had hardly even begun to fade when his second came up, and now it was impossible for me to stay there any longer, at least if I expected to find work and make good. The publicity against me had been just too adverse.

There was not one person in that whole town of three hundred thousand who didn't by now know my face, my name, and just about everything there was to know about me and my past, including my long involvement with Smitty. At least, they knew all they seemed to want to know about me, all of it bad, plus a lot of sordid fiction that certain newsmen had managed to dig up from some of my most devoted enemies about town.

I, a Squealer

Most of all, they knew and remembered Smitty's one and only defense—he couldn't have murdered the girls because I had murdered them.

Many people had actually believed this, or at least had believed it in part. After all, I was the one who had blown the whistle and had known where to find the bodies, and, apparently, the one who had known the most about the crimes. Smitty had forever maintained his innocence—and my guilt—in Gretchen's and Wendy's deaths. This was something the good people of Tucson would not soon be ready to forget.

In short, the city, its people, and its press had crucified me, and now I was trying to get away. In the words of Paul G. as he spoke them to a newspaper reporter prior to his departure from town, "I hate you, this city, its people, and its press. All I want to do is get the hell out of here." That was exactly the way I felt by this time.

I was traveling only a few miles, but those few miles made all of the difference in the world. Outside of where it all happened, and in a bigger, more active city such as Phoenix, the people would be far more removed from the murders and so much less concerned or preoccupied by them. But in Tucson it was an entirely different story. There, the stories of the murders were running rampant. This didn't surprise me in the least.

There is something that I have to say at this point about the town of Tucson. I just cannot allow it to go on blameless in any way. I do not believe these murders could have occurred in quite the same way anywhere else in the world—just in Tucson.

Only in this highly transient, unstable town (a one-of-its-kind, held together by God only knows what), which offers

Leaving

its young people nothing (no jobs simply because there's no industry, no place to go because there's no worthwhile teenage establishments around, and nothing to do other than cruise in cars, park and make out, or get in trouble), could a Smitty— this Smitty or another like him—take hold of the reins of so many and guide them blindly down such a path of destruction as he had done.

This city itself was what nurtured him, and for that matter, what nurtured all of us; this city had made him and all of this possible. I was happy now to be leaving it, although I knew inside I would be returning again. If I'd really wanted to leave it I'd have gone a thousand, two thousand miles away, but, magically, Tucson and all of its nothingness somehow still bound me securely to it so that I could never really leave.

That was the real tragedy of it. Tucson never releases its prisoners. They always come back, and they never know why. They just come, and all of their troubles start anew. I could name so many such cases, and to the best of my knowledge they're still there, struggling along, getting nowhere. And here I was, trying to leave.

I kissed my wife goodbye, went in and looked at our daughter sleeping soundly in her crib, and then left the house for the highway. Standing there with my thumb out to the passing cars made me remember another time of standing on the highway like this, on my way back from Chicago. That had been my first major attempt at getting away, but I'd been in such a hurry to get back that I'd hitchhiked the whole distance without stopping once, not even for the rain.

I'd rested only in the cars and while I was moving, moving

back toward the monotonous rows of houses that I was looking out across now from my elevated spot on the roadside, and from which I was waiting to leave all over again come the very first ride. I laughed and asked myself what would become of this trip, and how long would it last? "Home," I said. "You goddamned...."

A semi-truck swept by with a loud, whining sound, and I turned my back to avoid messing up my hair. I wanted to look as neat as possible if I expected to get a ride. Most of the creeps on the highway I wouldn't pick up myself. I wanted to at least look respectable.

I wondered how many of the people in the cars recognized me as they went by. The old lady sitting in the front seat would eye me, and as the car sped out of sight I imagined her turning in alarm to her husband at the wheel and saying, "That was Richard Bruns! Why, if we would have picked him up he'd have killed us. God, why do they let guys like that run loose?"

Why? Just what had I done to deserve all of this? I had turned Smitty in, done what I had to do, and I had blown the whole damn thing sky high. Hadn't that been the right thing? Why then were they giving me hell for it? I'd already been through enough hell. But now they asked, "If he didn't have anything to hide, or anything to do with it, then why hadn't he turned him in sooner?"

I wondered what the difference was since, in the end, I had turned him in. Couldn't they begin to realize how I had grappled with my conscience to do a thing forbidden to me as part of the code of youth—to betray, to squeal on a friend? I'd lived by that code for so long. And the code never changed regardless of the crime. Only the people involved could change, and I felt I had changed.

But now it seemed they didn't want me to change, that instead they wanted to make me into something worse than I had been before. So they called me a dope peddler, a gun runner, a pimp, a murderer.

Sometimes murder, this kind of murder, is like a disease. It infects an entire community, grows, and threatens to cripple the very fiber by which the populace functions as a whole. It feeds off of sensationalism and craves an unknown cure. The murders involving Charles Schmid had to become sensationalized. For years he had successfully functioned as the leader of teenage society of Tucson, and he had been trusted and admired by almost everyone—parents and teenagers alike. Yet he was to be arrested and tried for murder—not for the murder of just one person, but of three young girls.

The great metropolis of Tucson was in for a rude awakening. It would steadfastly refuse to accept it. As it would turn out, everyone was innocent of blame, with the exception of sixty (a number pulled out of someone's hat) unnamed members of a conjured-up sex club. No parents had been duped; none of their sons or daughters were involved. Smitty was cast in the role of president of the club which, it was said, was comprised only of a bunch of potheads, pushers, bootleggers, car thieves, muggers, purse snatchers, pimps, and, of course, murderers—all high school dropouts and reform school veterans. As the gossiping, speculating, and finger-pointing grew, I was cast in the role of vice-president.

I too had to share in the guilt. I was that mystery element

in the crime. I was the guy everyone knew was involved up to his neck but somehow managed to get away with it all and so was the one to attack the hardest, and attack they had. They had completely destroyed me. I was supposed to have been the good guy, but it hadn't worked out that way. I wondered if Smitty had this planned all along, too. In a way, he had still won.

Immediately after Smitty's arrest, reporters and writers from every corner of the globe had flocked into town. The welcome mat had been thrown out to them, and the townsfolk seemed to be in their glory. At no other time would so many people have so much to say about something of which they knew so little. Everyone had something to say or add to what someone else had said. Suddenly, everyone was an authority. As a result, the whole thing was blown entirely out of proportion, and the truth was buried somewhere under an avalanche of crap.

Rather than just accept the murders for what they had been—horrible tragedies to be learned from—people had to exaggerate and add to them (the sex club, among other things), to feed the national press reporting them, while of course protecting themselves at all times. But it had never occurred to them they were giving the city as a whole a black eye. All they had been able to see was that they had suddenly become the center of attention, and, so they had talked their heads off, and everyone suffered as a result of it. That was why I was leaving now.

A car speeding toward me began to slow, the single male occupant of it leaned forward over the wheel to scrutinize me, and then he pulled to a sudden and jerky stop about twenty-five yards past me. I turned and ran to the car, opened the front

Leaving

door, and looked in at a cleanly dressed man in his early thirties who asked, "How far are you going?"

"Phoenix," I answered.

"Well, I'm going as far as Coolidge if that'll help you."

"Sure." I jumped in and closed the door behind me. He shifted the car into gear and turned back out onto the highway. Soon Tucson disappeared behind us.

9

The Division Between Us

We talked about movies and movie-making throughout most of the trip. He was a projectionist at a local drive-in theater.

"I guess they'll be filming a movie on that Charles Schmid thing pretty soon," he remarked.

The story about the film had appeared in the newspaper several days before, accompanied by a picture of the film's producer. Apparently my host had no idea who I was, although he'd said, "You look awfully familiar. I know I've seen you somewhere before."

"I guess they're going to shoot the film in Tucson, too," he went on.

"Yeah, that's what I understand," I answered. "At least that's what the papers said."

It took probably forty minutes to reach our destination, and by that time the topic of conversation had managed to change. We drove all of the way through Coolidge—about a mile and a half from beginning to end traveling along the main thoroughfare. At the far edge of town he stopped and let me out, then turned and drove off into a residential area.

I, a Squealer

I set my grip down on the curb, propped one foot on the curb and the other in the street, and waited for a car to go by. Coolidge was just a little town of several thousand off of the main route to Phoenix. I waited and waited for a car, and was beginning to think that one would never come.

Across the street from where I was standing was a gas station, and caddy-corner was a diner. Just behind me, in a line, were three semi-trucks parked in the roadway, their drivers presumably at the diner getting a bite to eat. On my other side was a vacant field at the end of which was a National Guard Armory. Almost directly in front of me was a sign with the words, National Guard Armory, and an arrow pointing toward the large beige-colored building to the east. It was down the road leading to the armory, about fifty yards in front of me, that my ride had turned. It was lined with houses all of the way to the end, and midway down I could see the car I'd just stepped out of parked in the driveway of a home there.

It was about noon at the time and getting hot. I took my sport coat off and laid it over the top of my suitcase, lit a cigarette, took two or three drags off it, and then flicked it away because it was parching my throat. I decided that if I didn't get a ride soon I would cross over to the diner and have some lunch, get something cold to drink, and cool off.

Invariably I thought of Smitty. It occurred to me that he was also taking a trip today. He was being returned to prison from the Pima County Jail where he had been kept for the past couple of weeks during his second trial. He was to be going back home. I say "home" because, if blind justice has her way, he will live out the final hours, minutes, and seconds of his life there, until the moment that the cyanide capsule is dropped into the bucket of solution and the gas disperses into his lungs, when he will cease to breath and feel any longer.

Until then, that ugly stone fortress that stands at the edge of Florence, Arizona, would be his only home. Only if the Supreme Court, reviewing his appeals, were to later reverse his conviction in the murders of Gretchen and Wendy Fritz would he ever have hope of someday being set free again. Otherwise, he was returning to prison for the last time. He would never leave it again. At any rate, he was now the confessed murderer of Alleen Rowe, and for that he had received fifty years to life.

Yesterday I'd turned on the news and heard about Smitty leading a group of officers and morbidly curious onlookers to the desolate spot in the desert, pointing down and saying, "This is it." From that spot officers had unearthed the body of Alleen Rowe, who had been missing for more than two years.

He'd been grabbing at his last and futile straw. Claiming he'd been coerced into pleading guilty to the murder by his new attorney, F. Lee Bailey of Boston, he wanted to prove that the skull of the girl had never been fractured (the trial had taken place without Alleen's body ever having been found), thus shattering the police's contention that she'd been bludgeoned to death.

Then he undoubtedly hoped to shift the guilt over to John Saunders. It was possible, though not very likely, to beat someone over the head, kill her, and still not fracture her skull. But laboratory tests had shown Alleen's skull had been massively fractured, and so he'd lost this final attempt at proving his innocence, and from that moment had found himself with no other recourse to follow and nowhere else to turn.

Mary French and Saunders had both confessed to their roles in the slaying long ago, although they had failed for one reason or another to find the body. They both became witnesses against Smitty. It had been by Smitty's hand that she died. And so, Smitty dropped his coercion complaint, and his plea of guilty stood. Now it was written: He had forfeited his right to walk among us, and he was being returned to death row today, to remain possibly to the very end.

I couldn't help but feel deeply sorry for him. His crimes had been outrageous, but his punishment even more outrageous. I just cannot believe society has a right, morally or legally, to kill with premeditation another human being. And, on Death Row, dying is such a slow process.

Appeals and stays of execution to delay the moment, renewed hope upon renewed hope shattered into utter despair, and, finally, the last-minute countdown to the end; the fighting over, submission, in total hopelessness, is the only relief, the only peace. But then we haven't even the decency to permit the condemned this much. There's always the reprieve that never, never comes. It's all too harsh, too unmerciful. It simply cannot be just.

Pity must go out to Smitty's child bride of just several months, Diane. On the day it had begun, it was past her that the police had shoved to get to Smitty in the bedroom. Then they whisked him back past her again, handcuffed, to a waiting car outside.

She hadn't even fully grasped what was happening when they shoved him into the back seat of the car, and with her pleas and screams ignored, driven him away. Then had begun the ordeal of the waiting, the letter writing, the trials, and when it had all become too much, divorce.

She hadn't met Smitty until after Gretchen and Wendy disappeared, and so she'd been the most innocent of all. She hadn't even been a part of his past, yet it was his past, amid their new plans and dreams of the future, that would catch up and destroy them forever. The fortune-teller had been right when she told them one night after reading their palms, "Whatever you do you must never marry, because if you do your marriage will end in tragedy."

Perhaps if the fortune-teller had told me Smitty would never kill again, and given me a guarantee of it, I would have never had to turn him into the police—and perhaps I wouldn't have. But who can trust a fortune-teller?

Things happen as you'd expect them to happen in a novel or in a movie. The happy scenes, the traditional endings—the guy riding off into the sunset with his sweetheart. And sad, tragic stories ending just the opposite. My story is to end just that way — almost too poetic, too timely to be true. But still it happened.

I'd been standing there on the curb for close to an hour. In that time possibly twenty cars had gone by, with only one stopping; it had been going in the wrong direction. It had been going to Florence. Half a mile ahead of me was a fork in the road I hadn't realized was there, because of the trucks in the way, until that car had stopped. One of the roads in the fork, the right one, led to Florence, while the other went into Phoenix. I would be taking the road to the left.

I, a Squealer

Suddenly, a car came toward me from about two blocks away. I watched it get closer and closer, traveling slowly because of the town's speed limits. The car was white in color, and a late model; I guessed it to be that year's. I put my thumb out as it approached. When it was less than a block away, though, I pulled my thumb back again.

First I'd noticed the chrome spotlight sticking out from the window on the driver's side. Then I'd noticed the orange license plate it was bearing, designating it a government vehicle. There were three men in it, two in the front seat, and one in the back on the side closest to me. It could have been a cop car or any one of a number of different government agencies cars, but, whatever it was, it wasn't in the habit of picking up hitchhikers, unless possibly to take them to jail.

When it approached the street to the armory I looked in at the faces of the two men in the front. They were both young, in their early thirties, and I was sure they were both police. Then, as the car drew even with me, I looked in at the face of the young man in the back, and what I saw resulted in the most traumatic moment of my life.

My knees buckled, and I nearly dropped to the ground. My insides ripped, as if hands had torn through and pulled everything out, and were still there grabbing and yanking at whatever remained. The blood swelled to my head, my heart pounded, and a loud ringing filled my ears, deafening me.

It was Smitty in the back seat. It was Smitty, and he was just sitting there—sitting there staring out, seeing nothing. He'd looked right at me—me standing there watching him slowly go by—and he didn't even show a reaction; not so much as a flinch or an eye twitch. He looked right at me, but nothing happened. He hadn't moved. Nothing had registered. He just sat there as his eyes passed me and then fixed in the same position, stared out into the open field and then into the back of the first truck, and out into the open field again as he moved beyond my sight, obscured by the trucks.

I stood there, transfixed to the spot, unable to move, as my heart pounded—like a soul buried alive and trying to tear down the walls entombing it, like it was trying to break out of my body. And, as the car disappeared behind the first truck, I started for the street to chase after him, to get just one more good look at him before he was gone. Something inside of me demanded it, but my body refused to move and I stood still.

I just stood there, and he just sat there. His hands limp on his lap. He sat like something unearthly—hollow and empty, and removed. He sat, I would have sworn, a dead man. Then sounds, foreign sounds, were invading the deafness, penetrating into it, and suddenly I was aware of still another activity, and I jerked around, startled to see a car beside me, its motor running and its driver watching me curiously.

"You want a ride?"

A ride? I didn't answer.

"Where are you going?"

"Phoenix," I said.

"I'm going to Phoenix. Get in."

He reached across the seat to the door handle, pulled it down, and with a shove swung the door open for me. Slowly, as though calculating each move, I picked up my suitcase, stepped off from the curb into the street, and with three short strides walked the distance to the car. It was more of an inner awareness that caused me to react and perform, and my motions were more mechanical than deliberate. I swung my grip through the opening and into the back seat, stepped in and sat down, and grabbing hold of the armrest, pulled the door shut.

The car began to move, creeping away at first and then picking up momentum, and the flickers of white that were the broken lines in the center of the road passed with progressive speed until, out of the corner of the eye, they became like one continuous line. The trucks, the diner, the gas station, the final dwelling on the outskirts of the town were all left behind.

Now, I sat staring up at the white late model car at the top of an overpass, off to the right, in which another sat, also silent and motionless, staring out into a different scene—the vast flat field of ranches and wastelands that made up all of the surrounding countryside. As the miles passed even they, because of their immense expanse, became prison-like. There seemed to be no end to their desolation, and the further one journeyed into them toward their core, the more the feeling of entrapment and total solitude became until, before civilization were to again pop up from out of nowhere, they would become almost unbearable.

For Smitty, it must have been as though the earth itself were swallowing him up. And then the white car descended from the overpass and disappeared from sight just as the car in which I was riding veered sharply away, in just the opposite direction from him, and it was indeed as though the earth had swallowed him up.

The division between us had become complete.

10

Beginnings and Endings

"He said he wanted to kill someone, and he wanted to do it tonight," Mary French had told the court, "and he asked me if I would try to talk Alleen into going out with John."

She related how they drove to John Saunders' house. "John and Smitty got a shovel and put it into the trunk of the car. We drove around until Alleen's mother's car was gone." Alleen's mother worked nights as a nurse at a local hospital. "I walked through the alley and tapped on Alleen's bedroom window. Alleen came out the back door. She had on a bathing suit and a shift. Her hair was in curlers."

She told the court that they drove out to the desert. "The four of us got out of the car," Mary said, "we walked down to the bottom of the wash. We sat down and started talking. Somebody mentioned the radio, and Smitty asked me if I would go back up to the car and get it. Smitty and I walked back to the car together. We heard a scream. He said, 'She's in trouble.' Smitty went back down."

I, a Squealer

———— o ————

I remember Smitty telling me at the park that he and John made Alleen take off her bathing suit. He told me that they both had relations with her. First John, and then him. He told me, "If Mary ever found out I did anything to her, she'd kill me." He described to me what she'd been like, and what she looked like. He said, "We made her put her bathing suit back on again. First I tried to strangle her, but she wouldn't strangle, so I picked up a rock and bashed it over her head. Then I told John she wasn't dead yet and told him to hit her again. After he hit her, I told him, 'You killed her.'"

———— o ————

"About thirty minutes later," Mary continued testifying, "John came back to the car alone. John said that Smitty wanted me to come back down. I told him that he would have to come and get me himself. John went back down. About five or ten minutes later Smitty returned. He got in the car and said, 'We killed her. I love you very much,' and kissed me, and went to the back of the car and got the shovel. He was breathing real hard. He was excited. The next morning I found blood on my blouse where he'd touched me on my shoulder.

"I walked down to the wash with Smitty. Alleen was on the ground. She was lying on her back, and there was blood on her face and head. Her curlers were off, and she was all messed up. John and Smitty started digging. We gathered up her curlers. Smitty told me to take the shovel and dig. We dug with our hands. We put her in the grave, and then her shift. We buried the shovel and Smitty's shirt. They wiped the car clean of

Beginnings and Endings

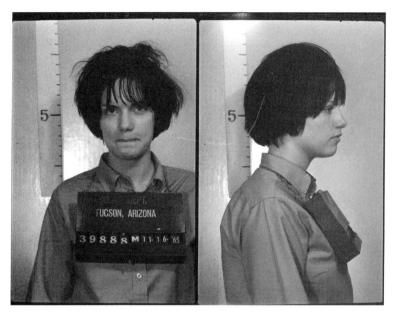

Mary French Arrest Photo / Tucson Police Department

fingerprints and took me home."

———————— o ————————

I had turned him in, and I'd done the right thing. Now it was over. It was now fully over. My nightmare was over. He'd gone his way, and I'd gone mine. Two roads, two different directions, two different people—two people once so very close, but now so very far apart, and the distance between us grew greater with each passing second.

On that very day when it had all begun, when the police had gone in and ripped him from his home and his freedom, it had been I who had gone in and confronted him in that little cell-like room. Now, with the last of his trials over, and his destiny spelled out before him, it was I, possibly the last free

I, a Squealer

man he'd ever again see in the free world, who stood almost at the prison gateway, as fate would have it, to witness his passing from society and from the world for the last time. I who had turned him in, and who had made this moment possible. I only thank God that I wasn't traveling that other route along with him.

But I'd gone the other way, and I was going the other way now. I was going out into the world, not alone, but with a beautiful wife and child at my side, while he was being returned to prison, to a place called Death Row. I was going out to face life with all of its strange and wonderful happenings, while he was going back to face death and damn each passing second that would bring him closer to it. I was going on with life, while he was being retired from it. The road went on and on. For Smitty, sometime during those next few minutes, the road came to a sudden and definite end.

Epilogue
(written in 1967)

The prevention of crime is the ultimate goal. If indeed Smitty is executed, as the law now says he must be, we will have taken one giant step backward from finding a solution through which we may later prevent other such murders as these from occurring. It is only through blindness and stupidity that we execute all of the Charles Schmids.

There can be nothing gained through vengeance, and the fact remains that punishment in itself is not a deterrent to crime. Rather, early detection and help is what is needed and called for, and called for desperately. But we must first learn the reasons behind this kind of troubled mind; where and how it begins, what specifically causes it, what cultivates and continues to feed it, and what is needed to curtail it before it is allowed to mature into a completely uncontrollable state that culminates in tragedy.

Only in this way can we save the mentally sick individual and at the same time spare the innocent. It is, in my opinion, high time we took the first step. Do not kill the Charles Schmids.

I, a Squealer

Charles Schmid 1965 / Arizona Daily Star

Study them, come to know and understand them, and they can supply vital answers we need in order to begin. They are our greatest assets and tools with which to work.

Do not kill them for even one ounce of retribution. Then we may be in a position to take that first major step forward. The time is already long overdue for reforming our concepts toward the criminally inclined—indeed, long overdue for revolutionizing our penal system as it now exists.

So we must recognize the need, find the initiative, and then take action toward change and reform. It is needed. It is needed to save the life of Smitty, a human being, who probably had no control over his actions to begin with.

Appendix 1

Charles Howard Schmid Jr. Timeline
March, 1966 through March, 1975

March, 1966:

Charles Howard Schmid Jr. is convicted of first degree murder for killing Gretchen and Wendy Fritz. He is sentenced to the death penalty. From an article in The Daily Star March 2, 1966:

Gas Chamber Decreed For Murders Of Sisters
JURY FINDS SCHMID GUILTY
Two Hours Taken For Verdict
By Pete Cowgill

An impassive Charles H. Schmid yesterday heard a jury find him guilty of murdering the teenage Fritz sisters and sentence him to die in the gas chamber.

The eight-woman, four-man Superior Court jury deliberated 2 hours and 10 minutes before reaching a unanimous verdict of guilty on two counts of first degree murder. The jury set Schmid's penalty at death.

I, a Squealer

Judge Lee Garrett will sentence Schmid formally on March 11 and set the date for his execution at that time.

Prosecutor William Schafer III said after the verdict that the state "definitely" will go ahead with the trial of Schmid on the charge of killing 15-year-old Alleen Rowe on March 15. Schafer was the prosecutor during the 11-day trial.

Defense Atty. William Tinney would not comment on the verdict. Asked if he planned to appeal, Tinney said, "I'm going home to dinner."

A few moments later he said, "I don't know about you, but I'm going home to see my wife and family."

Schmid, 23, was impassive when the clerk read the verdict before a packed courtroom.

His wife, Diane, 15, broke into loud sobs. He turned in his chair and waved at her to be silent as her uncontrolled sobbing filled the room.

The short, stocky, black-haired defendant leaned forward in his chair as the jury filed into the jury box. He was breathing rapidly and he squinted slightly.

Appendix 1

While the jury was being polled after both guilty verdicts were announced he rocked back and forth slightly, looked at reporters, court officials and the clerk who called the roll. He only glanced from time to time as each of the jurors affirmed the guilty verdict and the death penalty.

After the jury filed from the room Diane rushed up to Schmid and threw her arms around his neck. Several photographers jumped up to take pictures but Judge Garrett who had not retired from the courtroom admonished them and prevented any pictures being taken.

At the request of Tinney the defendant was allowed to leave the courtroom through the door leading to Garrett's secretary's office while he was on the bench. Only photographers outside the courtroom could take pictures of Schmid.

"You're a bunch of vultures—" a red-haired woman friend of Charles and Katherine Schmid, foster parents of the convicted killer, screamed at a group of photographers who were crowding around the family.

"You got what you wanted—now go," she shouted as the flashbulbs popped and reporters crowded around to catch a glimpse of Schmid's wife Diane who was slumped in a chair in the lobby outside the courtroom.

The defendant did not say a word in court except perhaps a whispered encouragement to his wife. His only words outside the courtroom were, "That's the way it goes."

With his hands cuffed behind him he was taken to a waiting car by Deputy Sheriff Henry Booth who has escorted the defendant and guarded him during the entire trial.

June, 1966:
Schmid is scheduled to be executed by lethal gas on this date, but the execution is postponed due to an awaiting appeal.

July, 1966:
A divorce between Charles and Diane Schmid is finalized.

May, 1967:
Schmid pleads guilty to second-degree murder for the death of Alleen Rowe and is sentenced to 50 years for her killing.

June, 1967:
Schmid, claiming that attorney F. Lee Bailey coerced him into pleading guilty to the murder of Alleen Rowe, takes police to the site where Alleen's body was buried in an attempt to prove his

innocence. He hopes to show that Alleen was not bludgeoned to death, thereby proving the prosecution's case wrong. The autopsy proves that her skull was massively fractured and Schmid's sentence stands.

1971:

A US Supreme Court ruling declares the capital punishment laws in Arizona unconstitutional. As a result, Schmid's death sentence for the murders of Gretchen and Wendy Fritz is commuted to 50 years in prison.

October 1972:

Schmid disappears from his maximum security cell. Roadblocks are set up and law enforcement searches inside and outside of the prison. He is found hours later hiding inside of a clothing locker in the prison welding shop. The clothing locker is a short distance from where a hollowed out gymnastics horse is found. It is believed that Schmid was transported to the welding shop inside of the wooden horse by fellow inmates.

November, 1972:

Schmid successfully escapes from prison with another triple murderer, Raymond Hudgens. Authorities believe that Schmid is heading to Tucson. Richard Bruns and his family are immediately put under police protection. The two fugitives take four hostages at gunpoint from a ranch house near the prison and drive to Tempe, AZ. They leave the hostages and split up. Both are recaptured within days: Schmid is discovered at a Tucson rail yard. In an attempt to alter his appearance he is found wearing a woman's blonde wig.

I, a Squealer

Schmid re-captured at rail yard in Tucson / Tucson Citizen

1974:

Schmid legally changes his name to Paul David Ashley. The reason, according to his Coolidge attorney, was that Schmid felt his old name hindered his efforts for rehabilitation.

March 20th, 1975:

Schmid is beaten and stabbed more than twenty times (some reports say up to 47 times) by two fellow prisoners. He is stabbed in one eye, one lung, is severely slashed in the abdomen and intestines, sustains a severed ureter, and numerous other wounds to the face, chest, and torso. As a result of the attack doctors remove Schmid's right eye and suture a damaged lung. He develops a blood infection and a tracheotomy has to be performed to aid in his breathing. His kidneys fail.

110

Appendix 1

March 30th, 1975:

At 12:30am—ten days after being attacked by fellow inmates—Charles Howard Schmid Jr. dies from his injuries at the age of 32.

Schmid's gravestone at Florence State Prison Cemetery

Appendix 2

Headlines & Sidelines

John Saunders pleaded guilty to second-degree murder in the killing of Alleen Rowe and received a life sentence. As reported in The Arizona Daily Star:

> **Saunders Gets Life for Rowe Murder**
> To Testify At Trial Of Schmid
> By Pete Cowgill
>
> A gasping, blinking, white-faced John Saunders was sentenced to life in the state prison yesterday for killing pretty 15-year-old Alleen Rowe.
>
> Saunders, 19, his hands clenched tightly in front of him, swayed erratically before the bench as Superior Court Judge John Collins pronounced the sentence.
>
> Collins could have sentenced Saunders to die in

the gas chamber as the youth had pleaded guilty to smashing the petite Miss Rowe with rocks until she died May 31, 1964.

Both Saunders and Mary R. French, also 19, are expected to testify at the murder trial of Charles Schmid Jr. next March 15. Schmid, 23, has pleaded innocent to the killing of Miss Rowe.

Saunders, dressed in a two-toned gray sport jacket, white shirt and tie, in a halting and barely audible voice told Collins, "I dedicate the rest of my life to make myself a better person to live with . . ."

W. Edward Morgan, the court-appointed attorney for Saunders, told the judge the defendant has had a complete reversal of his convictions. He asked that the youth's life be spared.

Collins said he was going to fit the punishment to the man, not the crime.

"There is a place in the bosom of the trial judge for mercy at the time of sentencing," the judge told Saunders.

"You have a deep religious background but when you needed it most, you did not use it," Collins said.

The judge told the youth that he was easily influenced by others and that he was the "passive party in this matter."

Saunders was told that psychiatrists said he could make a readjustment to lead a good life and do justice to the community if allowed to do so.

"You will probably never be able to get it (the murder) from your mind," Collins said, "but this is the way of the good Lord."

Collins said he was extending the wise hand of mercy in sentencing the tall, black-haired Saunders to life in prison rather than to death in the gas chamber.

The average time served in the state prison by persons given a life term on a first degree murder charge is from 12 to 15 years, according to Walter Hoffman, chairman of the State Board of Pardons and Paroles.

At Morgan's request, Saunders life sentence will start the day after Christmas.

Following the sentencing Morgan turned to the youth, wrapped his arms around him and said, "Now you can start a new life."

With newspaper and television photographers popping flashbulbs, Saunders embraced his father and mother. They whispered for several moments, nearly oblivious to the many pictures being taken in the courtroom after the judge left the bench.

Saunders was then handcuffed with his arms behind his back and led from the courtroom by two armed deputy sheriffs. He will be taken to the state prison at Florence on Dec. 26.

According to prison records, a John Saunders was released from Florence State Prison in 1990. If this is in fact the same John Saunders, he would have served approximately 15 years for his life sentence.

Mary French was sentenced to four to five years in prison. As reported in The Arizona Daily Star:

Mary French Sentenced To 4-5 Years In Prison

Displaying not a flicker of emotion, Mary Rae French, a slender, 19-year-old brunette, heard herself sentenced yesterday to spend four to five years in State Prison for being involved in the slaying of Alleen Rowe, 15.

Appendix 2

She stood silent and unbending as the sentence was passed but later she burst into tears as she walked down the stairway leading from the courtroom.

The teenager who was apprehended in Belton, Texas, on Nov. 14 received two concurrent sentences on charges of concealing and compounding a felony and being an accessory to the murder of the Rowe girl.

She had entered a plea of guilty to the charges on Nov. 25.

Superior Court Judge Robert Roylston told the former Palo Verde High School student that he could not give her probation which was urged by Jack Redhair, her court-appointed attorney.

Redhair told Roylston before sentencing that Miss French was only 17 years old at the time of the killing of Miss Rowe on May 31, 1964.

"She was under the influence of an older man (Charles Schmid, 23, also charged with the murder)—she loved this man and he told her not to tell of the crime—loved ones do not tell on each other," Redhair said.

The attorney claimed that Miss French did not

know there was going to be a murder until it happened. He said her only crime was in not telling of the murder after it happened. Following the slaying she went to Texas and severed her relationship with Schmid.

"When she was contacted by the police in Texas she told the whole truth about the crime," Redhair said. "She cooperated one hundred per cent."

Redhair pleaded for probation for Miss French for about 15 minutes. He claimed the girl should be rehabilitated rather than punished by putting her in prison. He said she should be given the opportunity to complete her high school education so that she can become a useful member of society.

Miss French stood with her head bowed at times before Roylston. The only thing she said was "No, sir" when the judge asked if she had anything to say before sentence was pronounced.

Roylston said he had received preliminary reports from the Adult Probation Office ever since the girl pleaded guilty. He had a very comprehensive report last weekend which included psychiatric reports, letters to and from the girl and various versions of the crime as told to the probation officers by Miss French and others involved in the murder.

Appendix 2

The judge said none of these reports are public.

The maximum sentence which could be given Miss French on each charge was five years. In pronouncing the sentence Roylston merely said he could not place the girl on probation and he then set the term at four to five years on each count to run concurrently. The actual sentencing took no more than 20 to 30 seconds.

French served her maximum sentence of five years in about three years because of work and good behavior time. By working she received one day "credit" for every day worked plus additional days for good behavior. She was released on December 28, 1968 and told reporters that she would be returning to her home town in Texas to attend college.

Francis Lee Bailey was retained by Schmid to assist William Tinney in the Alleen Rowe murder trial. At the time Bailey had just finished successfully arguing before the U.S. Supreme Court that Sam Sheppard had been denied due process, winning a re-trial. A not guilty verdict followed. The Sam Sheppard case inspired the television series, The Fugitive, and the 1993 movie of the same name. This case established Bailey's reputation as a skilled defense attorney and his arrival to Tucson created lots of local media attention.

Schmid ended up pleading guilty in the Alleen Rowe case, but later claimed he was coerced into pleading guilty by Bailey.

According to Bailey: "In short, once we impaneled a jury, the prosecution began to have doubts that it could get a second death sentence, and offered a non-capital plea. Schmid chose to take it, although since he was a total psychopath, I expected a blow-back, and therefore made a solid record of 'knowing and understanding waiver' of the right to jury trial in the plea allocution."

F. Lee Bailey went on to have many notable cases throughout his career. He was the supervisory attorney in the court martial of Captain Ernest Medina for the My Lai Massacre. Other high-profile cases included: Albert DeSalvo (The "Boston Strangler"), Patty Hearst, and O.J. Simpson.

Bernard L. Garmire served as Tucson's Chief of Police from 1957 through 1969. In 1968 he was described in *Life* magazine as a *"career lawman ... who ... followed his badge from city to city like the town-tamers of the Earp era ..."* At the time, Garmire was locked in a very public battle to rid Tucson of an influx of members of organized crime families from the East coast. His targets: criminals who, according to Garmire, had brought gangland violence to the quiet, dusty streets of Tucson. Garmire would win, thanks in large part to community engagement. According to Reader's Digest, *"In the true tradition of the West (Tucson) had organized the good men to drive the bad men out."*

He served as Chief of Police in Miami, FL from 1969 to 1975, and interim Chief of Police of Paradise Valley, AZ in 1986. Garmire passed away in Phoenix, Arizona on July 8, 2011 at the age of 96.

The Bonanno Crime Family is one of the five major New York City organized crime families of the Italian American Mafia. They are most recently known for the infiltration by FBI agent Joseph Bistone aka Donny Brasco. For over 30 years the family was one of the most powerful in the country. It was in 1931, after mob boss Salvatore Maranzano was killed, that Joe Bonanno was awarded most of Maranzano's crime family. At 26 years old, Bonanno was the youngest mafia leader in the nation. Bonnano directed his family into illegal gambling, loan sharking, and narcotics. The family built significant interests in California and Arizona. He also expanded into Canada.

On October 21, 1964, Joe Bonnano disappeared for almost two years. After months of no word from Bonnano, Gaspare DiGregorio was named the new boss. The family split into two factions, the *DiGregorio Supporters* and the *Bonanno Loyalists*. The media referred to this as the *"Banana Split"* or *"Banana Wars"*. In 1966, DiGregorio arranged for a meeting between the two factions in Brooklyn. When the Bonnano Loyalists arrived a large gun battle ensued. The DiGregorio Supporters had planned to wipe out the Bonnano Loyalists, but failed, and no one was killed.

In May 1966, Joe Bonnano reappeared and rallied a large part of the family to his side. The war between the two factions

I, a Squealer

was brought to a close when Joe suffered a heart attack and announced his retirement in 1968. He went on to live to the age of 97, dying in Tucson in 2002. There have been six official bosses to the Bonanno crime family since Joe Bonnano retired. At the time of this writing Michael "The Nose" Mancuso is the official boss.

Charles Joseph Battaglia known as *"Charlie Batts"* was a soldier in the Los Angeles crime family who later switched allegiance to the Bonanno crime family. In the 1960s, in Tucson, there were at least ten bombings that were linked to the mafia. Informants told law enforcement that Charlie "Batts" Battaglia ordered some of the bombings. In the late 1960s Battaglia was imprisoned in Leavenworth for extortion. During his time in prison authorities intercepted messages from Battaglia to Bonanno suggesting they divide Arizona; with Battaglia taking Phoenix and the northern part of Arizona and Bonanno taking Tucson and the southern part of Arizona. Both mobsters were charged with conspiracy based on these messages, but were acquitted after one witness disappeared and the other was discredited. Battaglia died of natural causes on March 1, 1983 in Phoenix at the age of 66.

The Northeast Blackout of 1965 (mentioned in chapter 6)
The largest blackout in the history of the United States, happened on November 9, 1965. A disruption in the supply of electricity was caused by human error—maintenance personnel incorrectly set a protective relay on one of the transmission lines—affecting parts of Connecticut, Massachusetts, New Hampshire, New Jersey, New York, Rhode Island, Pennsylvania,

Appendix 2

Vermont, and parts of Ontario in Canada. Over thirty million people and 80,000 square miles were left without electricity for up to 13 hours.

The blackout became the inspiration for storylines in books, movies, and songs including; *Rosemary's Baby* (novel by Ira Levins), *Underworld* (novel by Don DeLillos), *Where Were You When the Lights Went Out?* (film starring Doris Day and Robert Morse), *Where Were You When the Lights Went Out?* (song by Tom Paxton), *Strangers in the Night* (song by heavy metal band Saxon), and the topic of the blackout was written into countless television series.

Life **magazine** was an American magazine that ran from 1883 to 1972 and again from 1978 to 2000. It featured the Charles Schmid murder cases in its March 4, 1966 issue. Don Moser, the writer of this article, gave Schmid his "Pied Piper of Tucson" nickname. It was this article that is credited for putting these murder cases into the national spotlight and creating the inspiration for several fictional works based on the people and events. Because the article was an unflattering portrayal of Tucson it left many Tucson residents upset.

Appendix 3

2017 Interview with Richard Bruns

How did your friendship with Smitty first start?

We would see each other at the "Sunset Rollerama" roller skating rink, where they had dances with national headliners like The Drifters and Fats Domino, but it was just in passing. Then one afternoon I was at Thrifty drug store talking with a mutual friend when Smitty came into the store and joined our conversation. Afterward I was walking home and Smitty drove up beside me and asked if I wanted a ride. He drove me home and we started hanging out regularly after that.

You indicate in your description of your relationship with Smitty that you were friends for several years, despite his flaws. What drove your desire to continue to be friends with him even though he was a con artist and had a volatile personality?

Well, he went downhill. He wasn't a creep when I first met him. He was the guy that everybody wanted to be around. I can remember being at Tucson High School which was an open campus. There was a street that ran right in the middle of the high school between the cafeteria and the athletics department, and I remember him driving down there at lunchtime in a red Chevy convertible and everybody running to his car. He wasn't wearing a patch over his nose and painting his face. He was a cool guy back then. By the time he had evolved, I'd become quite afraid of him.

Can you go into detail about your fear of Smitty when it came to Kathy?

He kept giving me reasons to fear for Kathy. When I was with him I didn't have to worry about where she was. But when I wasn't with him, then I got this panic; which drove me onto her street, which drove everybody on the street crazy, and they all thought I was nuts—maybe I did go a little nuts.

I can remember being on Kathy's street early on in my vigil. I was walking on the sidewalk when all of a sudden I saw his car turn the corner onto her street and I ducked behind some hedges. I don't know why I ducked, because I had no reason to hide from him, but I did. He stopped his car about a house away from Kathy's. He got out and walked onto Kathy's lawn and then walked up to Kathy's bedroom window. He meandered around there a bit and then got back into his car and drove off. I was scared shitless that he was going to see me in his rear view mirror crouching down and hiding. I would have absolutely no way in the world to explain to him why I was hiding from him. It wasn't the first or last time I saw him on her street, which just

Appendix 3

reaffirmed my suspicions.

You share that Smitty was aware that you were watching over Kathy. Since he didn't know you were trying to protect her from him, why did he think you were watching over her?

He understood and appreciated my watching over Kathy because he was obsessive and jealous in his own relationships. As far as he was concerned, if a girl was in a relationship with him, she belonged to him, so my assumed obsession with Kathy was something he could relate to. I was doing his thing.

By allowing him to believe that I was keeping her captive in her home because I was jealous and didn't want her seeing other people, I had him believing that I was as crazy as he was. In this way it was easy to hide my true motives in watching over her. As long as he believed I was crazy too, he could trust me. I was good at getting him to trust me, but at that point we were the opposite of friends.

Do you think he knew that you were the opposite of friends?

No. I did a good job, but I also realize that he was playing me too. I have no doubt now that he had plans for framing me all along.

Can you elaborate on that?

Looking back and knowing what I know now, I can see that

there was a way for him to commit the perfect series of murders and get away with it. If he had picked me up one night and killed me. And then, later that same night, went to Kathy's window and coaxed her to go out with him, killed Kathy, and then buried the two of us in the same spot (which, by the way, if he had buried us where Alleen Rowe was buried, that area is still undeveloped today), our bodies would have never been discovered.

The next day, when Kathy came up missing, who would have been responsible? Richard would have been responsible. Everybody would have unanimously agreed that Richard was the person responsible. Sometime later the bodies of Gretchen and Wendy would have been discovered, along with my fingerprints, and I would have been blamed for it all.

Do you believe that was his plan?

He had enough foresight to make sure I left evidence at the gravesite by throwing Wendy's shoe, which was black patent leather, so it must have left a nice pristine fingerprint. Then my sunglasses came up missing. They were found later near the bodies, which didn't make sense because the only time I went out there was that night with Smitty and I wasn't wearing my sunglasses. Then, the night that Gretchen and Wendy went missing, Gretchen's car drove by my house. I was sitting outside in a friend's car when we saw her car driving down my street and then make a u-turn to head back the other way. We couldn't see who the driver was, but I've often thought it must have been

Sunglasses found at the grave site of Gretchen and Wendy Fritz
Tucson Police Department

I, a Squealer

Smitty driving by to pick me up. If I'd gotten into her car that night my fingerprints would have been in her car. When he saw me with someone else he must have decided to get out of there. And then the evening of my court date, in which I was ordered to leave town, I was riding in a friends car up north of the city when Smitty came from behind and honked for us to pull over. He stopped behind us after we pulled over and then walked up to the passenger side to talk with me. He asked me how my court date went. It never made sense that he was at that same spot which was way north of the city. He had to have been following me. I told him that I had to leave for Columbus, Ohio the next day. That must have irked him to no end, if in fact he had been planning to kill me and Kathy, thereby making me the perfect patsy for all of his murders.

You say that Smitty confided that he killed four times, not three. Did he ever share any specific details about a fourth murder with you?

No. I remember during the trials hearing rumors about a guy he might have killed, but he never shared anything about that with me.

It seems that every article or story ever written about Charles Schmid mentions his stuffed boots. As his friend were you aware that he was stuffing his boots to appear taller?

I was more surprised than anyone when that information came out. I had no idea. I knew he had a peculiar walk, but I thought it was just the way he walked.

Thinking back, can you ever remember a time when you saw him without his boots on?

Never. In fact I remember one time in particular that I went with him to a local boot maker because he wanted to have some custom Beatle boots made. The boot maker asked Smitty to take his shoes off so that he could trace his feet for the pattern, but Smitty refused. Smitty had me take my shoes off and had the guy use my feet. Well, of course, once the boots were finished they didn't fit Smitty. He ended up giving me the boots, which was a good deal for me since they were expensive, custom boots. I thought it was odd that he refused to take his shoes off that day, but I never gave it too much thought.

In the trial for the murders of Gretchen and Wendy Fritz, Smitty's defense was that you were the murderer. What types of questions did you have to face on the stand?

Well, just to show that I'm not biased, I don't believe Smitty had a completely fair trial. As soon as his defense attorney started to raise those types of questions with me, the judge stated, "Mr. Bruns is not on trial here," and shut that line of questioning down. I remember Smitty getting upset and throwing his pencil. I was prepared to answer anything they asked, but I didn't end up having to answer any of those types of questions.

You share that you attempted to find work in Phoenix to

I, a Squealer

distance yourself from the trials, but you ended up staying in Tucson. How long after the trials did it take for the negative backlash toward you to calm?

It never did—and I never understood that. Everybody assumed that I was a criminal. Everybody assumed I did jail time, when in fact I've never spent a second of my life in jail. I've never been booked. I've never had my mug shot taken. I've never been fingerprinted. I was just a witness. All I did was help to take a killer off of the streets of Tucson, and potentially save a girls life, and for that I've been raked over the coals.

It affected every job I ever had. While I did eventually find steady work, the backlash continued. Even in my mid-forties, when I went back to school to get my teaching degree at the University of Arizona, they found out who I was and put me through an inquisition before I was allowed to continue in my studies. I'm still pretty pissed off about the whole thing.

When you look back on the period of the 1960s, and compare that period to today, what kinds of changes in the youth do you see?

When I think back to the 60s, I feel like young people were looking for something outside of themselves. I think that the war had something do with that. There was a lot of fear, and young people were looking for purpose or something to believe in. I think that opened up opportunities for people like Charles Schmid. Shortly after, you had Charles Manson. I don't believe

'GIVE ME A CHANCE'

Man Who Tipped Police To Tucson Murders Seeks Help

By NICKI DONAHUE
Citizen Staff Writer

Richard L. Bruns, the man who tipped police about the crimes of condemned murderer Charles H. Schmid Jr., is appealing to U.S. Rep. Morris K. Udall for help in burying the past.

Bruns, now married and the father of three little girls, has just been fired for the third time in a year because "they won't ever give me a chance."

Now 23, Bruns has no criminal record, other than a misdemeanor trespassing charge after he pleaded guilty to keeping a day-and-night watch over a 15-year-old girl he believed Schmid had marked as a victim.

"I know now it got ridiculous," he says, "and looking back, I know I was insanely obsessed, but I had to do the things I did."

Through the years, since Schmid was sentenced to die for the murders of Wendy and Gretchen Fritz and to life imprisonment for the murder of Alleen

Richard L. Bruns

Rowe, Bruns has looked for work

But usually, he said, "when they find out who I am, I get fired."

His last job, with a local automotive parts company, required that he be bonded. But before the application for bond could be processed, the company's local manager was ordered by a superior in Phoenix to let him go.

Bruns, who also has lost jobs at a local print shop and bakery, told Udall: "I need people such as yourself with powerful voices to help me through this mess. I can no longer go on butting my head against a wall.

"I know there isn't much you can do, but if you would write a letter to this company (the automotive parts firm) maybe they would let me keep my job."

For some 18 months, Bruns drove a delivery truck for the Westerner Flower Shop, 3348 E. Speedway. He left that job for a higher paying one.

"Of course, we had a qualm when we hired him," said Mrs. Harry J. Stith, wife of the owner. "But we have never had a finer employe."

Said her son, James:

"He was one of the best employes we ever had. This poor guy has the worst luck of anyone I ever met. I can't blame him for wanting a better job than he had with us. We can't pay a large salary. He only wants to better himself and support his family. We will recommend him to anyone, any day."

Bruns is training at the American Institute of Technology to be a computer programmer. He is also buying a small home.

"But even when I finish school, will anyone hire me?" Bruns asked today. "I've borrowed money to attend this school. Any job I get will require a security clearance. Will I ever be able to get it even if I do find someone to hire me?

"There are many people in this world who started out with the wrong friends and associates but went on to live a meaningful life. Why can't I have a chance to do the same?"

"I've tried and I've worked hard," Bruns wrote to Udall, "and I only want to be like anyone else. Why can't people stop being so petty and give me and my family a real chance."

Because he said he was conscience-stricken, Bruns led authorities to the bodies of the Fritz girls in a desert area in the Catalina Mountain foothills. He said Schmid had shown him the bodies after boasting of killing the girls.

"Someday," Bruns said, "there'll be another young man that this town will need as it needed me, and he, too, will have to search his conscience and make a decision. He may look back at what has happened to me, shudder, get sick and go right on being silent."

"I'm at the point where I can't go on without help . . . I just can't cope with this thing any more."

today people like Charles Schmid or Charles Manson would have the attraction they had back then.

Did you ever see or speak with Kathy, Paul, or Smitty again?

I ran into Kathy a number of times, but we never spoke. Paul once made a delivery to a print shop I worked at. We saw each other but never spoke either.

Like I wrote in my account, while I was hitchhiking to Phoenix, I saw Smitty being transferred to Florence Prison. To me, that was quite traumatic. It was literally like we came to a fork in the road; he on his way to life in prison, and me onto my new life. I guess that's the end, isn't it?

We know what happened to Smitty. What were the highlights of the past fifty years for you?

I have three beautiful daughters and three wonderful grandchildren. They are my highlights. For my seventieth birthday I went to Six Flags Magic Mountain with two of my daughters and one of my grandsons to ride the roller coasters. I was definitely the oldest person there, so I consider myself fortunate.

———— o ————

From Fact to Fiction

From the time the world first learned about Charles Schmid and his young victims, a number of writers and film-makers have found creative inspiration in the sensational facts and people surrounding the cases. Following are some of the most recognized:

Where Are You Going, Where Have You Been?
by Joyce Carol Oates

This short story first appeared in the Fall 1966 edition of Epoch Magazine. According to interviews with Oates, she was reading the March, 1966 *Life* magazine article on the Schmid cases and sensed immediately that there was potential for a story of her own. She stopped reading halfway through the article so that her imagination could take over and let the fiction develop independently of the facts.

Smooth Talk
1985 Coming of age / Indie film

Directed by Joyce Chopra and starring Laura Dern and Treat Williams. This film was loosely based on Joyce Carol Oates' short story, "Where Are You Going, Where Have You Been?" It received the Sundance Film Festival Grand Jury Prize.

I, a Squealer

The Lost

(Leisure Books / 47 North) by Jack Ketchum.

According to Ketchum: *I first read about Charles Schmid in J. Robert Nash's "Bloodletters and Badmen," an excellent encyclopedia-style reference book on American murder. The piece on Schmid included a photo of him grinning rakishly for the press, arrogant as hell. It stuck with me. Some years later I got to thinking about the Vietnam era, the guys who went to war and those who stayed home. Charlie would have stayed home.*

The Lost

2006 Psychological horror film

Written and directed by Chris Sivertson and based on Jack Ketchum's novel of the same name.

Half in Love With Death

(Simon & Schuster/Merit Press) by Emily Ross.

Named a finalist for best YA novel in the International Thriller Writers Organization's 2016 Thriller Awards. When asked about the inspiration for her YA novel, Ross writes: *When I started my novel "Half in Love with Death," I knew I wanted to write about a young girl who falls for a guy who is not what he seems to be. My sister suggested I base him on Charles Schmid—a man she confided had fascinated and terrified her ever since she'd read a Life magazine article about his story in 1966. Once I read the article and learned more about Schmid, the charmer whose beguiling blue eyes hid a monster within, I knew I'd found the inspiration for the deceptive young man in my novel.*

Acknowledgements

This book would have never come to life if not for the passion and commitment of my daughter Lisa. Thank you.

I'd like to thank the Arizona Daily Star and the Tucson Citizen for their courtesy in allowing us to utilize their articles and photos. A special thanks to Johanna Eubank for the resources she offered through her Tales from the Morgue series, and thank you to the director of photography, Rick Wiley, for his time.

The Tucson Police Department was very helpful in tracking down information and photos.

Thank you to Aimée Carbone and José Olivas with the RBDI Group for their time, commitment, and creative input.

I appreciate editor, Susan Ferguson, for proofreading without changing my original writing.

And finally I am so grateful to the many authors who gave their valuable time to read and offer comments, advise, and support. I am impressed by the generosity that exists in the world of writers!